VOLUME

9

THE
AMERICAN HERITAGE
BOOK OF THE
PRESIDENTS
AND FAMOUS AMERICANS

★ ★ ★ ★ ★

WOODROW WILSON

WARREN GAMALIEL HARDING

CALVIN COOLIDGE

CREATED AND DESIGNED BY THE EDITORS OF
AMERICAN HERITAGE
The Magazine of History

12-VOLUME EDITION PUBLISHED BY
DELL PUBLISHING CO., INC., NEW YORK, N.Y.

Woodrow Wilson

Warren Gamaliel Harding   *Calvin Coolidge*

CONTENTS
OF VOLUME NINE

FAMOUS AMERICANS

WOODROW WILSON

It was the early evening of September 15, 1910, and the scene was the Taylor Opera House in Trenton, New Jersey. A lean man with iron-gray hair and slate-blue eyes behind glittering, rimless glasses was being helped through a mass of admirers toward the stage door. "God! look at that jaw!" exclaimed an onlooker. He was getting his first glimpse of Thomas Woodrow Wilson, president of Princeton University and the man the Democrats of New Jersey had just nominated as their candidate for governor.

Not all the Democrats assembled in Trenton that evening were elated over the choice. Wilson was the candidate of Newark and Jersey City political bosses, and the progressives at the convention awaited his acceptance speech with sullen suspicion. The determined thrust of his jaw, which so startled the man at the stage door, should have been a warning to the bosses and progressives alike that Woodrow Wilson was not going to be the candidate of any faction. He was then, as ever after in his spectacular political career, his own man and his own man only. "I did not seek this nomination," Wilson said in his acceptance speech. "It has come to me absolutely unsolicited." If elected, he promised, he would be free to serve uncommitted by any prior pledges. This personal declaration of independence brought the progressives at the convention roaring to their feet. "Thank God, at last a leader has come!" one of them reportedly shouted.

It was a curious, twisting road that had led Woodrow Wilson to the New Jersey gubernatorial nomination in 1910. The candidate—and future President of the United States—had been born on December 28, 1856, in Staunton, Virginia. His father, Joseph Ruggles Wilson, was a native Ohioan of Scotch-Irish stock and had been a printer and a teacher before becoming minister of

Woodrow Wilson, portrayed by John Singer Sargent in 1917

In 1883, the year this picture was taken, Wilson enrolled at Johns Hopkins as a graduate student.

Staunton's First Presbyterian Church. Jessie Woodrow, his mother, was the daughter of another Presbyterian minister and had been born in England. A year after the birth of their first son, the Wilsons moved to Augusta, Georgia.

Woodrow Wilson later said that his first recollection was of hearing, when he was only four, that Abraham Lincoln had been elected President and that there would be war. The next few years were stamped with the bitter events of the Civil War and Reconstruction in Georgia and in South Carolina, to which his family moved in 1870. Three years later, Wilson enrolled at Davidson College, a small Presbyterian school in Piedmont, North Carolina. He was only sixteen, a frail and timid youth away from home for the first time. He left Davidson after only one year and spent the next fourteen months regaining his health.

In September, 1875, he entered the College of New Jersey, at Princeton. An intense and hard-working student, Wilson excelled at debate and oratory during his undergraduate years. Daydreaming of the political career to which these talents might lead, he wrote out on cards one day: "Thomas Woodrow Wilson, Senator from Virginia."

Upon his graduation from Princeton in 1879, Wilson entered the University of Virginia Law School. But frail health once more cut short his formal education, and he completed his law studies at home. In June, 1882, he started to practice law in Atlanta and the following October was admitted to the Georgia bar.

Young Wilson's path took an important turn when, in the fall of 1883, he entered graduate school at Baltimore's Johns Hopkins University. Less than two years later, in January, 1885, his first statement of political philosophy, *Congressional Government*, was published to unanimously enthusiastic reviews. The book submitted the constitutional system of checks and balances to a practical, political scrutiny and found it sorely lacking. It was Congress, wrote Wilson, that was dominant. The United States would be better served by its elected representatives, he suggested, if Congress reorganized itself along the British cabinet system, whereby the majority political party in the House of Commons provides a Prime Minister and cabinet members from among its own ranks. The President, he wrote, was nothing but an ineffective figurehead.

While still basking in the prominence that publication of his book had brought him, the graduate student was married in June, 1885. He had met his bride, Ellen Louise Axson, two years earlier in Rome, Georgia. The couple's first home was at Bryn Mawr College in Pennsylvania, where, that fall, Wilson took up the duties of associate professor of history. In June, 1886, he was awarded a Ph.D. from Johns Hopkins and for two more years continued to teach the fashionable young ladies at Bryn Mawr, a job he began to find tedious. His salary was only fifteen hundred dollars per year.

After two more years of teaching—at Wesleyan University in Middletown, Connecticut—Wilson was offered, and enthusiastically accepted, a full professorship of jurisprudence and political economy at his beloved alma mater, Princeton. Steadily he built a towering reputation in academic circles. In addition to his work at Princeton, he lectured at New York Law School, continued his studies at Johns Hopkins, and by 1902 had published nine scholarly volumes and thirty-five articles. Three times in these years he was offered the presidency of the University of Virginia and each time declined—as if waiting for another, more challenging opportunity. It came on June 9, 1902, when the board of trustees of Princeton unanimously elected him president.

Wilson's tenure at Princeton began with several notable triumphs. He was successful in reorganizing Princeton's course of studies and its departmental structure and in introducing the preceptoral system of education. Then in June, 1907, he launched an attack on Princeton's eating clubs, which he felt emphasized social rather than intellectual values. Wilson proposed to substitute a system of quadrangles, wherein the students could live and eat as well as study together. At first the trustees approved Wilson's plan. But when the school's alumni violently objected, the trustees backed down, and Wilson—in a preview of a later crusade to win people to his viewpoint—appealed over their heads. Traveling around the country, he undertook to explain his plan to members of various alumni clubs. He failed to rouse a following, however, and the next year the quadrangle plan was dropped. During the

last two years of his presidency a more serious struggle developed over the location and control of a graduate school. The issue—a largely independent graduate school located off campus versus a subordinate institution on campus—seems trivial today. Yet at this time Wilson dramatically demonstrated the stubborn refusal to compromise that was to lead to his greatest defeat as President of the United States. He wanted the graduate school under his control, on campus; he saw the issue as a test of his power and prestige, and he was prepared to resign if he did not have his way. Wilson turned the dispute into a mortal contest between democracy and the forces of special privilege. The latter, in his somewhat curious viewpoint, would be served by a separate, aristocratic graduate school. The increasingly bitter fight raged on for two years and ended anticlimactically in June, 1910. A several-million-dollar bequest to Princeton rested on the establishment of an independent graduate school, off campus. Wilson, swallowing his pride, accepted the money and the battle was over. By that time, however, university affairs no longer held much interest for him, and the following October 20 he resigned. The philosopher and scholar had caught the political bug.

"It is immediately, as you know, the question of my nomination for the governorship of New Jersey," Woodrow Wilson wrote a friend the month of his defeat in the graduate-school controversy, "but that is the mere preliminary of a plan to nominate me in 1912 for the presidency."

The plan had been developing since 1906, when Colonel George Harvey, influential editor of *Harper's Weekly*, had boldly proposed the Princeton leader as the Democratic candidate for President—if not in 1908, then in 1912. In the fall of that year there was talk of Wilson running for United States senator from New Jersey in 1907, and Princeton's president cocked an attentive ear. The bosses of Newark and Jersey City thought they had found a perfect front man, but when progressive Democrats in the state announced that they would fight Wilson's

Princeton Tiger

As the cartoon above illustrates, Wilson's tenure as president of Princeton had its stormy moments.

nomination, he withdrew from the race rather than compete in what promised to be a sordid struggle.

In 1908 the Democrats nominated William Jennings Bryan for President for a third time. Although remaining a loyal Democrat, Wilson refused to share a speaker's platform with Bryan. "[He] is the most charming and lovable of men personally, but foolish and dangerous in his theoretical beliefs," Wilson told a reporter. Bryan's defeat by William Howard Taft that November removed the most powerful obstacle to a Wilson presidential candidacy in 1912. Clearly the Democrats would need a fresh face at the end of the next four years.

Curiously enough, Woodrow Wilson, regarded as generally conservative, was himself searching for a fresh identity. Along with Bryan's noisy campaigns, Theodore Roosevelt's Presidency had set the entire country to thinking about progressivism. But, in Wilson's opinion, neither Bryan nor Roosevelt was a successful reformer. "We must now stop preaching sermons," he told a St. Louis audience in March, 1909, "and come down to those applications which will actually correct the abuses of our national life, without any more fuss, and without any more rhetoric."

The following October, Wilson was elected president of the Short Ballot Association, a national group that believed that reduction of the number of elected city officials would lead to more efficient and responsive municipal government. Woodrow Wilson took up this cause as he did all his involvements—he made it a crusade. At Colonel Harvey's suggestion, Wilson next turned his attention to the Republicans' highly protective Payne-Aldrich Tariff. Soon thereafter he was swinging out against the trusts.

The New Jersey political bosses who had wanted Wilson as their candidate for United States senator in 1907 now urged him to run for governor in 1910. His speeches and arti-

cles were making him a widely known, popular figure. His political innocence would no doubt make him a cooperative partner, the bosses believed. His philosophy, as far as they were concerned, was of minor importance. An intermediary wrote to the Princeton president in June, 1910, offering him the gubernatorial nomination. The bosses had "not the slightest desire" that Wilson commit himself "in any way as to principles, measures or men," the man wrote. They only wanted a pledge that if elected governor, Wilson "would not set about fighting and breaking down the existing Democratic organization and replacing it with one of [his] own." Wilson, who apparently had only a vague notion of what party organizations were, easily gave the pledge. The nomination at Trenton's Taylor Opera House followed in due course.

"I never before appeared before an audience and asked for anything," he apologized in his first purely political address. But Wilson soon warmed up to campaigning. And on November 8 he won 34,000 more votes than the combined total of his Republican opponent and several minor candidates.

Wilson's governorship must be classed as one of the most successful in New Jersey or

NEWARK Evening News

A New Jersey newspaper cartoon (right) applauded the initiation of Governor Wilson's reform program with the caption "Good Lord! He Really Meant It!"

any state. Even before his inauguration on January 17, 1911, he moved to declare his independence from the bosses who had nominated him. One of them, James Smith, Jr., of Newark, decided to seek re-election to the Senate seat he had held without distinction in the 1890's. At the time, United States senators were still elected by state legislatures, but Wilson had advocated making the results of the recently instituted party primaries binding on the legislators. He exerted great pressure on Smith, who had not even entered the primary, to retire from the senatorial contest. When the Newark boss refused, the governor-elect moved with skill and speed to line up supporters in the legislature. By the end of December he had enough votes to defeat Smith, and when the legislature assembled the next month, James E. Martine, the primary victor, was quickly elected. Thus, from the very outset of his political career, Wilson was indelibly marked as a progressive and an independent.

The new governor immediately drafted a program of reform on which he intended to base his entire administration. It consisted of four measures: direct primaries and election reform, legislation against corrupt practices, a workmen's compensation law, and regulation of public utilities. By April, bills pertaining to all four issues had been passed by the legislature, despite opposition by the bosses. But in the fall 1911 elections Wilson fought a two-front war and lost. Machine candidates defeated Wilson progressives in the Newark Democratic primary. And, on November 7, the Republicans surprisingly captured control of both houses of the New Jersey legislature.

Wilson's record with the 1912 session of the New Jersey legislature was nearly as dismal as his 1911 record was bright. He vetoed fifty-seven measures, revealing once again the tragic flaw in his character: an utter inability to compromise with opponents. "He had to hold the reins and do the driving alone," historian Arthur Stanley Link wrote in *Wilson: The Road to the White House;* "it was the only kind of leadership he knew."

Wilson's impressive electoral victory in 1910 and his record of accomplishment in the first year of his governorship had made him a leading contender for the 1912 Democratic presidential nomination. But despite his tireless pursuit of the endorsement in speaking tours that crisscrossed the continent in late 1911 and early 1912, the nomination was by no means Wilson's for the asking. In a series of primary victories James Beauchamp "Champ" Clark, the Speaker of the House, demonstrated that he had captured Bryan's agrarian following in the Midwest and Far West. A second candidate, Oscar W. Underwood of Alabama, chairman of the House Ways and Means Committee, was busily wrapping up state delegations in the South. By March, 1912, Wilson was writing gloomily to a political friend that Clark, Underwood, and Governor Judson Harmon of Ohio were conspiring to block his own nomination. On April 9 Clark defeated Wilson in the Illinois primary by a ratio of 3 to 1. "The back of the Wilson movement was broken yesterday in Illinois . . ." a Newark newspaper declared.

In November, 1911, Wilson had met "Colonel" Edward M. House, a wealthy Texas politician, who would develop an irrepressible yen to be a President maker. From the very first, the two found themselves in almost complete accord. Within a year their friendship ripened into an intellectual intimacy that has few if any equals in the history of American politics. Although House was never to hold elective or appointive office under Wilson, he in time became second only to the President in the Wilson administration. Feared and distrusted as the *eminence grise,* or power behind the throne, at the White House, House retained Wilson's full confidence almost till the end. "Mr. House is my second personality," Wilson once confessed. "He is my independent self. His thoughts and mine are one." But this communion of spirits was a thing of the future in 1912. Far from being President maker of that campaign, House was one of the first to look about for other candidates when the Wilson boom collapsed.

When the Democratic convention met at Baltimore on Tuesday, June 25, Champ Clark was the leading contender, with some 435 votes. A two-thirds majority—726 of the 1,088 delegates—was needed for the nomination. With only 248 votes pledged to his candidacy, the most Wilson could hope for was an alliance with Oscar M. Underwood or one of the other minor candidates that would give him the 363 votes necessary to block Clark.

The nominations got under way during the night of June 27. As predicted, Clark led the first ballot with 440½ votes; Wilson was second with 324; Harmon third with 148; Underwood fourth with 117½. Not until the tenth ballot, on the afternoon of June 28, was there any significant change in the voting. Then Tammany Hall delivered all 90 New York votes to Clark. But the expected band wagon failed to get rolling; Wilson and Underwood delegates stood fast, and the convention once more adjourned.

On the fourteenth ballot, on June 29, Bryan announced that he could no longer back Clark, who had been endorsed by Tammany, and was therefore shifting his support to Wilson. But again no landslide developed. The voting continued through Monday, July 1. On the thirtieth ballot Wilson passed Clark, but was still 266 votes short of the two-thirds majority.

The deadlock was finally broken on Tuesday, July 2, when Illinois switched to Wilson on the forty-third ballot. Several states, including Wilson's birthplace, Virginia, followed the Illinois lead, and on the forty-sixth ballot, Underwood released the delegates pledged to him. Harmon's men were also released, and Wilson, with 990 votes, was declared the Democratic nominee for President of the United States.

The Republicans, meeting two weeks earlier in Chicago, had renominated President William Howard Taft. That summer Theodore Roosevelt organized a third party, the Progressive or Bull Moose party, which nominated him in August. It would be the first real three-way contest for the Presidency since 1860. Yet, by mid-August, it

was generally agreed that the contest was between Wilson and Roosevelt; Taft was on the side lines. The portly President sat on his front porch, but sedentary campaigning was not for the dynamic Roosevelt or, finally, for Wilson. At first disdaining long public-appearance trips as undignified, Wilson soon found himself drawn more and more into active campaigning. Moreover, he found that not only was he good at stumping but that he actually was enjoying it.

The climax of Wilson's campaign came on October 31 with an address to a nearly hysterical throng at New York's Madison Square Garden. "What the Democratic party proposes to do is to go into power and do the things that the Republican party has been talking about doing for sixteen years," he shouted. "There is a very simple way of doing it—to direct the provisions of your law against every specific process of monopoly which has by crushing competition built up the control of small numbers of men, and then direct the punishment against every individual who disobeys the law."

On November 5 Thomas Woodrow Wilson was elected the twenty-eighth President of the United States. The final tally was: Wilson, 6,296,547; Roosevelt, 4,118,571; Taft, 3,486,720. (Socialist Eugene V. Debs received nearly a million votes.) Taft won only 8 electoral votes, Roosevelt 88, and Wilson took the remaining 435.

Perhaps the most important event of the 1912 presidential campaign was a quiet meeting, on August 28, between Wilson and Louis D. Brandeis, who was to help shape what came to be known as the New Freedom. That day Wilson entertained Brandeis, one of the nation's most outstanding progressive lawyers; the two talked through lunch and for three hours thereafter.

Brandeis was the formulator of a philosophy of government regulation of competition as a curb against monopoly. He wanted to sweep away monopolies by eliminating all the measures of government that bestowed special privileges on special interests. He wanted to restore completely the freedom of competition that he felt was the basis of

America's greatness. Wilson's career, from the presidency of Princeton through the Presidency of the United States, is the story of a basically conservative man's slow but certain conversion to progressivism. The meeting with Brandeis was one of the most important factors in that conversion.

The New Freedom, as preached to Wilson by Brandeis and later articulated in the campaign by the candidate himself, took shape in a number of far-reaching and important reforms by the new Democratic administration after Wilson's inauguration on March 4, 1913. A downward revision of the tariff, the first major overhaul of the American protective system in sixty-five years, was the principal item of business. Throughout the nineteenth century high duties on European imports had been imposed by the federal government to protect America's fledgling manufacturers. But as American industry thrived, such duties, by keeping out lower-priced goods from abroad, had a tendency to raise the American cost of living to an unnaturally high level. This government-sponsored protection of industry came to be looked upon as a subsidy to business, paid out of the pocket of the consumer.

To underline the importance he attached to tariff reform, Wilson called Congress into special session on April 7 and the next day dramatically appeared in person to address a joint session—the first President since John Adams to do so. The purpose of Wilson's appearance on Capitol Hill, he said in the tariff address of April 8, was to demonstrate that the President "is a person, not a mere department of the Government hailing Congress from some isolated island of jealous power, sending messages, not speaking naturally and with his own voice—that he is a human being trying to cooperate with other human beings in a common service."

Exactly one month later, on May 8, the House passed the Wilson-supported Underwood tariff bill, and the measure went to the Senate. Not yet popularly elected, members of the Upper House were considered by many to be representatives of special interests rather than of the people. The Seventeenth

EUGENE V. DEBS

In 1912 Eugene V. Debs was the presidential candidate of the Socialist party for the fourth consecutive time. Long before his conversion to socialism in 1895, Debs had been an important force in the labor-union movement. A fireman on the Terre Haute and Indianapolis Railway, he helped to organize the Brotherhood of Locomotive Firemen in 1875, becoming a national officer five years later. As president of the American Railway Union, which he helped to found in 1893, he led its members in a sympathy strike against the Chicago Pullman Company in 1894. Arrested and sentenced to six months in prison, Debs became acquainted with the writings of Karl Marx and emerged from jail a socialist. In 1897 he founded the Social Democratic Party of America, which three years later became the Socialist Party of America. After Debs had urged opposition to the war with Germany and had publicly denounced the sedition policy of the government, he was sentenced to ten years imprisonment in 1918. In spite of his confinement he headed the Socialist ticket for the fifth time in 1920 and polled more than 900,000 votes. Pardoned by President Harding in 1921, Debs spent his last five years in the service of his party. He was an editor of two Socialist journals, *Appeal to Reason* and *American Appeal*, and author of a book on prison conditions, *Walls and Bars*, published posthumously in 1927.

Amendment to the Constitution, providing for direct election of United States senators, was in the process of being ratified by the state legislatures, but would not be adopted until May 31, 1913.

That summer the long and often heated debate on the Underwood bill droned on in the Senate despite the efforts of Wilson and his supporters to achieve quick enactment of the reform considered the keystone of the New Freedom. Finally, on September 9, the senators voted. But when they passed the bill, by a seven-vote margin, it not only lowered duties 4 per cent below the House version but it also included a progressive income tax. Earlier attempts by Congress to tax incomes had been declared unconstitutional by the Supreme Court. The Sixteenth Amendment, providing for a federal tax on incomes, had been passed by Congress in 1909, but had not been ratified by the states until February, 1913. Those who linked the income tax to tariff reform argued that any duties on imports whatsoever unfairly taxed the consumer. Revenue to support the government should be based on the accumulation of wealth and not on the consumption of goods. It was apparently a persuasive argument with senators about to face popular elections for the first time. In retrospect, the passage of this first income tax law is seen as the most enduring legacy of the 1913 tariff reform.

While the battle for tariff revision was still raging, Wilson undertook a second and even more important fight. "It is absolutely imperative," he announced to a joint session of Congress on June 23, 1913, "that we should give the business men of this country a banking and currency system by means of which they can make use of the freedom of enterprise and of individual initiative which we are about to bestow upon them [by tariff reform]. We are about to set them free; we must not leave them without the tools of action when they are free."

It is difficult for subsequent generations, accustomed to a sound and stable currency

A mass meeting of the Industrial Workers of the World was held in New York on May Day, 1914 (above). Organized in 1905, the I.W.W. wished to abolish wages and organize industrial unions as the basis of a workers' government. The group's influence was lessened by its refusal to support the war effort in 1917.

rigidly controlled by the federal government, to imagine the chaos that marked American banking and currency before Wilson. In 1913 the country's seven thousand banks were only loosely controlled by Washington, and they operated without any real coordination among themselves. Even worse, there was no uniform currency but rather a miscellaneous collection of gold and silver coins, certificates, greenbacks, and National Bank notes.

Champion of the conservative viewpoint was Representative Carter Glass of Virginia, chairman of the House Banking Committee. The day after Christmas, 1912, Glass had visited the President-elect at Princeton to present his proposal for a system of independent, privately controlled reserve banks. Such a decentralized system, Glass argued, would take banking control out of the hands of Wall Street interests. Wilson appeared to go along with Glass, suggesting only that the system of reserve banks be coordinated by a government board. The board, Wilson remarked, would be but a capstone to Glass's system and not by any means the central bank the Virginian opposed. In subsequent months Glass and his supporters worked out an elaborate banking structure that would have given control of both banking and currency to private bankers. The President meanwhile was coming under increasing pressure from Brandeis and other progressives to place control of the system firmly under the federal government.

For six months after his second address to Congress, Wilson was occupied almost exclusively with the struggle for banking and currency reform. "Now it is the currency I have tackled," he wrote to a friend that June. "Not an hour can I let it out of my mind." On December 23, 1913—almost a year to the day since he had first discussed the matter with Representative Glass— Woodrow Wilson signed into law the act creating the Federal Reserve System. Glass's plan for independent, regional federal reserve banks was preserved, but they were to be regulated by the Federal Reserve Board appointed by the President and not includ-

Wilson composed speeches on this typewriter, which could be adapted to type either Greek or English.

ing, as Glass had wanted, bankers. Through the long fight Wilson and his progressive supporters had conceded nothing vital.

Tariff and banking reforms, then, were the principal achievements of the New Freedom. In other areas Wilson indicated that his halting journey along the road to progressivism had not really taken him far from his conservative starting point. The President refused to endorse a federal child-labor law introduced in the House early in 1914 because he felt it was unconstitutional. Although he had seemed to favor woman suffrage during the 1912 campaign, he repeatedly held off delegations of suffragettes with the excuse that failure of the Democratic platform to endorse the vote for women prevented him from supporting the measure. With his approval, white and Negro workers were segregated in government offices. And in 1913 he backed down on appointing Brandeis to his Cabinet (either as Attorney General or Secretary of Commerce) in the face of outraged protests from conservatives and anti-Semites. In 1916, however, he appointed, and won the confirmation of, Brandeis as an associate justice of the Supreme Court.

Wilson enjoyed being President. He had the self-confidence and dedication of a man who felt himself not only uniquely endowed but perhaps divinely ordained to hold the highest office in the land. Such a bold egotism was to make possible his early triumphs in the Presidency; it was also to lead to his tragic failures later.

He once confessed, in an address to members of the National Press Club, that "my constant embarrassment is to restrain the emotions that are inside of me. You may not believe it, but I sometimes feel like a fire from a far from extinct volcano, and if the lava does not seem to spill over it is because you are not high enough to see into the basin and see the caldron boil." But few people were to see behind the austere façade Woodrow Wilson presented to the world. It has been his fate to be remembered by the American people as one of the least lovable of their Presidents.

In 1962, four decades after Wilson's death, the publication of his love letters to Ellen Axson during their engagement revealed a new, unexpectedly passionate side of the man's personality.

Twenty-six-year-old Woodrow Wilson had caught a first glimpse of the woman he was to marry during a church service in Rome, Georgia, in April, 1883. Within six months they were engaged to be married, and he wrote in a rush of emotion "how passionate love grew rapidly upon me; how all my thoughts used to center in plans to win you; what castles my hopes used to build and how I used to sicken at the prospect of hope deferred; and then how, much sooner than I had dared to hope, how by a seeming accident, we met and you gave your heart to me, it all seems so like a sweet dream that I am afraid to credit my memory."

To Ellen alone he revealed himself. In one memorable letter he related that he had awakened laughing from a joyous dream. "Can you love me in my every humour?" he asked, "or would you prefer to think of me as always dignified? I am afraid it would kill me to be always thoughtful and sensible, dignified and decorous."

"I would have you catch a glimpse of my purpose for the future," he wrote Ellen three days before their wedding on June 24, 1885, "and of the joy which that future contains *for me*, of the gratitude I feel for *your* priceless gift of love, and of the infinite love and tenderness which is the gift of my whole heart to you. . . ." The touching message was to be his last letter to her, he believed, for after the wedding he would never allow her to be separated from him for a single day.

Woodrow, Ellen, and their three daughters—Margaret, Eleanor, and Jessie—made the White House a happy home. Two of the Wilson girls were married during their father's Presidency: Jessie on November 25, 1913, to Francis B. Sayre of Williams College; and Eleanor on May 7, 1914, to William G. McAdoo, Secretary of the Treasury in President Wilson's Cabinet.

Eleanor's wedding turned out to be one of the last public appearances the First Lady was to make. The preceding March she had fallen in her room and seemed to recover rather slowly from the accident. It was not until several months later, when it was too late to do anything, that her illness was diagnosed as tuberculosis of the kidneys and Bright's disease. At the end of May, 1914, she became bedridden, and on August 6— five days after World War I had erupted in Europe—she died. Gently releasing his wife's hand, which he had been holding in a bedside vigil, Wilson went to a window, stared out, and cried, "Oh my God, what am I to do?"

The man most deeply concerned by Wilson's seemingly incurable depression following Ellen's death was the White House physician, Dr. Cary T. Grayson. Wilson had inherited the Virginia doctor from Taft, and the two had quickly become intimate friends. It was Grayson who had urged the President to take up golf and who was his constant companion at regularly prescribed visits to the links.

In October, 1914, only two months after Ellen Wilson's death, Dr. Grayson introduced an attractive Washington widow, Edith Bolling Galt, to the President's cousin, Helen Woodrow Bones, then serving as White House hostess. In March, 1915, Miss Bones invited Mrs. Galt, by then a close friend, to tea at the White House. Wilson arrived unexpectedly with Grayson, and the two men joined the ladies for tea. A few days later, Wilson invited Mrs. Galt to dinner and shortly thereafter began taking long drives with her.

On May 4, he proposed marriage, but Mrs. Galt asked him to wait. Two weeks later she joined the official party aboard the presidential yacht, which was reviewing the Atlantic fleet in New York Harbor. "I feel like I [am] living in a story—and fear to move, lest I wake up and find it a dream . . ." she wrote. In September, she accepted Wilson's proposal.

"She seemed to come into our life here like a special gift from Heaven," Wilson wrote to a friend, "and I have won a sweet companion who will soon make me forget the intolerable loneliness and isolation of the weary months since this terrible war began." On December 18, 1915, the two were married quietly at Mrs. Galt's home in Washington, D.C.

"It would be the irony of fate if my administration had to deal chiefly with foreign affairs," Woodrow Wilson had said to a friend shortly before his inauguration. The 1912 campaign for the Presidency had been waged exclusively on domestic issues, and his mandate from the electorate was for progress and reform at home that would leave little time for matters beyond America's shores. Yet Wilson was to be faced with more immediate and far-reaching international problems than any of his predecessors. Almost from his inauguration in March, 1913, until his retirement eight years later in March, 1921, he was to be confronted with an unending series of foreign crises for which there were no precedents nor easy solutions.

In selecting his Cabinet, Wilson had no alternative to naming William Jennings Bryan Secretary of State. The long-time leader of the party, casting aside personal ambition and forgetting former slights, had loyally supported Wilson both in the convention and in the campaign; his considerable following of progressives was instru-

THOMAS R. MARSHALL

"Democrats, like poets, are born, not made," cracked Thomas R. Marshall, two-term Vice President of the United States. A loyal member of the Democratic party, Marshall was politically influential, but held no public office until 1908, when the fifty-four-year-old lawyer was elected governor of Indiana. During his four years in office he opposed rigid prohibition laws and pushed forward an important program of social and labor legislation. Presented as a favorite-son candidate at the Democratic convention of 1912, he was given the second spot on the ticket after the presidential nomination went to Woodrow Wilson. As Vice President, Marshall brought wit and humor to the routine task of presiding over the Senate. During one particularly wearisome debate, while a senator droned on about the needs of the country, Marshall turned to someone nearby and made his famous remark: "What this country needs is a really good five-cent cigar." The Vice President's role was complicated after 1918 by President Wilson's long illness. While the President lay incapacitated some members of the government felt that Marshall should assume Wilson's office; but the Constitution was not specific on the matter, and the Vice President was unwilling to appear to be a usurper. Thomas Marshall left office in 1921. In 1925, the year in which he died, he published his *Recollections*, a humorous account of his life.

mental in tipping the balance in Wilson's favor. Although the appointment of Bryan caused dismay among Wilson's more sophisticated and conservative supporters, the two dissimilar leaders got along quite well in the initial stages of the administration. Yet the President must have winced at the humorous uproar over Bryan's banishment of liquor from all diplomatic functions and the introduction of what the newspapers came to call "grape-juice diplomacy."

But Wilson had chiefly his own naïveté to blame for the long and ultimately unsuccessful imbroglio with Mexico. Applying his personal Calvinistic standards of right and wrong, he authorized American military intervention in the complex and largely misunderstood Mexican Revolution. By 1917, when United States troops were finally withdrawn, he had succeeded in doing little more than embittering United States-Mexican relations for decades to come.

But it was the outbreak of World War I in August, 1914, that was to lead to Wilson's most agonizing trials, his supreme triumphs, and—finally—his deepest tragedy.

Enduring the personal anguish of his first wife's illness and death, Woodrow Wilson was able to do nothing to mediate the international crisis. He did insist, however, on American neutrality. Setting this course for the United States, and keeping to it for the next two and one-half years, were to test all President Wilson's powers of leadership and perseverance.

At first the United States was probably as neutral as possible. Certain ties of history, language, and culture made most Americans favorably disposed toward Britain and France. On the other hand, large and vociferous minorities of Irish-Americans and German-Americans were either unrelentingly hostile to the British or openly sympathetic to Germany and Austria-Hungary. Throughout the period of uneasy American neutrality, there were a number of clashes with Britain but none that would have led to war. The introduction of unrestricted submarine warfare by Germany in early 1915 was the element that most sorely

THE WHITE HOUSE COLLECTION

Edith Bolling Galt, portrayed in a painting by Adolph Muller-Ury, was forty-three years old when she became the second Mrs. Woodrow Wilson.

tested, and eventually defeated, Wilson's efforts to keep America on the side lines.

The first major crisis resulted from the sinking, by a German U-boat on May 7, 1915, of the British Cunard liner *Lusitania*. Among the 1,198 who went down with the ship were 128 Americans. In one of the most unfortunate speeches of his career, three days later in Philadelphia, Wilson seemed to articulate a policy of peace at any price that was widely interpreted as cowardice. "There is such a thing as a man being too proud to fight," he said. "There is such a thing as a nation being so right that it does not need to convince others by force that it is right." Nevertheless, through successively stronger diplomatic protests to Germany, Wilson won his point. On September 1, 1915, Germany announced that it would not attack unarmed passenger liners.

In November, 1916, Wilson was narrowly re-elected to a second term on the campaign slogan "He kept us out of war."

He received 9,127,695 votes to the 8,533,507 of his Republican challenger, former Supreme Court Justice Charles Evans Hughes. The electoral vote was so close, however, that at first it appeared Hughes had taken California and thus the election.

Hughes, the story goes, went to bed on election night thinking he had been elected. When a reporter tried to reach him early the next morning with the news that he had lost California, an aide loftily said: "The President can't be disturbed." "Well," replied the reporter, "when he wakes up tell him he's no longer President." The closeness of the vote led the Republicans to hope for a recount that would reverse the outcome, and Hughes did not send a telegram conceding the election to Wilson for two weeks. Dryly commenting on the delay, Wilson said of the telegram: "It was a little moth-eaten when it got here but quite legible."

Despite its narrowness, Wilson interpreted his victory as a mandate from the people to act as international peacemaker He started by asking the opponents to state their war aims. The Germans refused to do so, and the Allied response indicated a determination to fight to the finish. Thus rebuffed by the belligerents, Wilson went before the Senate on January 22, 1917, to deliver his clarion call for a "peace without victory." The Senate cheered Wilson's noble sentiments; Robert La Follette called the address "the greatest message of a century." But un-

known to the President, Germany was already taking steps that made America's involvement in the war inevitable.

Shortly after 4 P.M. on January 31, 1917, the German ambassador arrived at the State Department to keep an appointment with Secretary of State Robert Lansing, who had replaced Bryan. Tears welled in the German's eyes as he delivered the diplomatic note announcing that his country would resume unrestricted submarine warfare the following day. All the concessions President Wilson had wrung from Germany since the *Lusitania* was sunk in mid-1915 were at one stroke abrogated.

Four days later, on February 3, in another speech to Congress, Wilson announced that he was severing diplomatic relations with Germany. He made one last effort to stay out of the war. Hoping to avoid a confrontation with Germany, he asked Congress for permission to arm United States merchant ships against submarine attack. By a lopsided vote of 403 to 13, the House passed the armed ship bill on March 1. In the Senate, however, eleven members, led by La Follette of Wisconsin and George Norris of Nebraska, filibustered until the session's end

President Wilson, to the delight of his wife (who is seated at his right), smilingly carries on the tradition begun by William Howard Taft as he opens the 1916 American League season by throwing out the first baseball.

This painting of Marines in France was done by a Marine artist-historian, Captain John W. Thomason, Jr.

on March 4, the day before Wilson's second inauguration. Wilson raged at the action of what he called a "little group of willful men," but immediately got a ruling from the State Department that he had authority to arm merchant ships entering the war zone without the consent of Congress.

The same day the House was voting, the State Department released for publication an intercepted telegram from German Minister of Foreign Affairs Alfred Zimmermann to the German ambassador in Mexico. The inflammatory message had been decoded by experts in London. In the event of war between Germany and the United States, Zimmermann had signaled, Mexico was to be offered an alliance and given assistance in regaining from America lost territory in New Mexico, Texas, and Arizona. Mexico was to urge Japan to join her in the attack on the United States. As sensational as the Zimmermann telegram was, it took several more sinkings of merchant ships, with the loss of American lives, to drive Wilson over the brink.

On the evening of April 2 Wilson went before a special session of both houses of Congress to ask for a declaration of war against Germany. The President reviewed his efforts to maintain neutrality and commented bitterly on Germany's increasing disregard for

that neutrality. "There is one choice we cannot make, we are incapable of making," he said to those who might still hope to avoid hostilities, "we will not choose the path of submission. . . . We are glad now that we see the facts with no veil of false pretense about them," he continued, "to fight thus for the ultimate peace of the world and for the liberation of its peoples, the German peoples included: for the rights of nations great and small and the privilege of men everywhere to choose their way of life and of obedience. The world must be made safe for democracy." The Senate, by a vote of 82 to 6 on April 4, and the House, by 373 to 50 two days later, approved the declaration of war.

Woodrow Wilson, ironically, is not remembered for the war he won but rather for the peace he lost. He proved wise in his choice of the man to lead the American forces in France, General John J. "Black Jack" Pershing—and wise in his determination that Pershing's American Expeditionary Forces should fight as an independent unit alongside the Allies.

America was sadly unprepared for the vast undertaking of a foreign war, and more than a year passed before United States troops entered the fighting in division strength. Meanwhile, in the spring of 1918, Germany launched a series of initially successful offensives that nearly defeated the Allies. At Château-Thierry and Belleau Wood in June, however, the doughboys helped stop the Germans, and that summer Americans contributed substantially to the Allied counteroffensives that turned the tide.

Secret negotiations for peace were already under way when Wilson appealed to the voters on October 25, 1918, to elect Democrats in the forthcoming congressional elections as an endorsement of his wartime policies. But Americans were already tiring of Woodrow Wilson and his war; on November 5 the Republican party gained control of the House by 47 votes and of the Senate by 2 votes. Six days later World War I came to an end.

Just a week after the November 11 armistice, Wilson announced that he would lead the United States delegation to the peace conference in Europe. On frequent trips to Europe in the preceding four years, Colonel House had been perfecting a role he loved to play, that of Wilson's personal and confidential emissary—at first offering the President's mediation between belligerents and after April, 1917, representing him among the Allies. Hearing of Wilson's intention to attend the peace conference, House cabled him from Paris: "Americans here whose opinions are of value are practically unanimous in the belief that it would be unwise for you to sit in the Peace Conference. They fear that it would involve a loss of dignity. . . ." Such a trip would also be a startling break with tradition. No American President had ever left United States territory during his term in office. Wilson was adamant. He would head the delegation to Paris. Since any treaty that came out of the peace conference would have to pass the United States Senate, Wilson was urged to include Republicans in the delegation. Inexplicably, he refused, announcing that the party would include, in addition to himself, only Colonel House, Secretary of State

The friendship between the capable, faithful "Colonel" Edward M. House (right) and Wilson became a casualty of the President's fatigue and ill health.

Lansing, General Tasker H. Bliss (United States representative on the Supreme War Council), and Henry White, a former diplomat, nominally a Republican but one with no political influence.

In a memorable address before Congress the preceding January 8, President Wilson had outlined fourteen points as the basis for peace. Eight of the famous Fourteen Points pertained to territorial adjustment after the war. Others called for open treaties and open negotiations of treaties, freedom of the seas, removal of economic barriers and equality of trade, reduction of armaments, and impartial adjustment of colonial claims. The fourteenth—and as far as the President was concerned the most important—related to a league of nations.

In his insistence on going to Europe, in all the negotiations at Paris, and in his subsequent fight to get the Treaty of Versailles through the Senate, President Wilson revealed that the League of Nations was of such intense importance to him that he was

willing to sacrifice everything to obtain it.

On December 4 the President and Mrs. Wilson sailed from New York on the liner *George Washington*. In France, in Britain, in Italy, Wilson received tumultuous receptions from war-weary populaces; they served to reinforce his growing conviction that he was the apostle of peace who represented the people of the world. It did not take him long after the formal opening of the peace conference in Paris on January 18, 1919, however, to realize that he would have to fight for that vision. Most of the work was conducted by the "Big Four"—Wilson, Lloyd George of Britain, Georges Clemenceau of France, and Vittorio Orlando of Italy. The other three were quietly contemptuous of the President: many of Wilson's points directly contradicted their secret treaties, and they were unwilling to surrender the territorial concessions contained in those agreements. The only thing the three seemed to agree on was a desire for vengeance on Germany.

In the subsequent months of negotiations Wilson time and time again conceded on matters of substance to maintain his one guiding principle: the League must be a part of the treaty.

In mid-February he returned to America to sign important measures before the adjournment of Congress. At an otherwise cordial dinner meeting with members of Congress, he failed to convince Republican opponents of the necessity for the League. Republican Senator Henry Cabot Lodge, a white-bearded patrician from Massachusetts, was emerging as the leader of the opposition. On March 2 he was among the thirty-nine Republican senators—enough to block Senate approval of ratification—who signed a round-robin resolution opposing the League as Wilson had outlined it and demanding that the League not be incorporated in the treaty.

Two days later, just before sailing again for Europe, Wilson spoke at a New York rally and hurled defiance at the senators. Upon his return with the completed treaty, Wilson predicted, the senators would not only find the Covenant of the League of Na-

In this drawing by Edouard Requin, the "Big Four" sign the Versailles Treaty; from left to right are Georges Clemenceau of France, Wilson, David Lloyd George of Great Britain, and Vittorio Emanuele Orlando of Italy.

tions included in it, they would find "so many threads of the treaty tied to the Covenant that you cannot dissect the Covenant from the treaty without destroying the whole vital structure."

Back in Paris, Wilson concentrated even harder on the League, to the exclusion of almost all other important items of business—including what to do with the upstart Bolsheviks who had seized power in Russia in November. In April, Wilson suffered an attack of influenza, which many later felt marked the beginning of a long decline in his mental and physical powers. He grew suspicious and resentful of House's role and even came to believe that his long-trusted adviser was betraying him.

The political wrangling at the conference grew worse, the meetings often verging on barroom brawls. At one point, the President had to step between Lloyd George and Clemenceau, who were about to exchange blows. Wilson threatened once to leave the conference, and Orlando actually did withdraw temporarily after the American President had appealed over his head to the Italian people. Wilson was scarcely on speaking terms with his French hosts by the conference's end.

Only two dejected, politically inconsequential Germans could be found to sign the treaty of vengeance on June 28, 1919. From a seat near Edith Wilson in Versailles's glittering Hall of Mirrors, Mrs. House jumped up to see her husband sign: "Please let me stand long enough to see my lamb sign." That was the last day on which Wilson was ever to see or speak to her "lamb"; the friendship was beyond repair.

Two days after his return to the United States on July 8, Wilson offered the Treaty of Versailles in an address to the Senate. "The stage is set, the destiny disclosed . . ." he concluded. "We can only go forward, with lifted eyes and freshened spirit, to follow the vision. . . . The light streams upon the path ahead, and nowhere else."

Most of the members of the Democratic minority in the Senate supported the treaty and the League of Nations, and they would

WOODROW WILSON HOUSE

Poland awarded Wilson its White Cross medal (above) for his efforts to promote an enduring world peace.

follow faithfully Wilson's leadership in the subsequent fight over approval of ratification. The Republican opponents, however, were split into two factions: a moderate group led by Lodge, who wanted to ratify a peace treaty and worry about the League later; and the "irreconcilables," such as La Follette, Idaho's William E. Borah, and California's Hiram Johnson, who rejected the League out of hand.

In September, 1919, Wilson—realizing he lacked the votes in the Senate—appealed directly to the people. Traveling nearly ten thousand miles through the Midwest and West, he delivered some forty speeches in thirty cities between September 4 and 24. At Pueblo, Colorado, on September 25, he stumbled while stepping up to the speaker's platform. But he went on to deliver an emotional oration that brought tears to many eyes and that he concluded with tears streaming down his own face.

That night Wilson suffered what probably was a slight stroke. The months and years of his wartime Presidency, the six-month-long ordeal in Paris, the frustrations upon his return to Washington, the grueling tour —all had taken their toll. The remainder of the trip was canceled, and the presidential train rushed back to the Capital. There, on October 2, Wilson had a second, far more severe stroke that left him partially paralyzed.

For the next seven months the President was almost a recluse in the White House, cut off from most contacts with the outside world and attended principally by the faithful Dr. Grayson, his private secretary, Joseph Tumulty, and Mrs. Wilson.

Much has been written—mostly unfavorable—about Edith Wilson's role during the President's invalidism, and she has been called the nation's first Lady President. In her memoirs she confessed that she had acted, at the doctors' advice, as a screen around her husband, judging just what messages from congressmen and Cabinet members should be brought into the sickroom. When she emerged with verbal instructions or a document with an illegible scrawl that purported to be her husband's signature, no one was able to say just who was making the decisions.

Congress sent a delegation to determine whether Wilson was truly incapacitated. Vice President Thomas R. Marshall fretted about being asked to take over, and Secretary of State Lansing, after he convened and presided over a Cabinet meeting in Wilson's absence, was dismissed.

These same months witnessed the culmination of the fight for the treaty and the League in the Senate. On November 6 Lodge announced that he was for ratification but with—ironically—fourteen reservations. In a letter from the sickroom on November 18, Wilson directed his supporters to reject Lodge's reservations, and the .Democrats joined the irreconcilables in voting against an amended treaty on November 19. Unconditional acceptance was then defeated by the moderate Republicans.

Subsequent attempts to revive the treaty in the early months of 1920 failed, and on May 20 Congress passed a joint resolution declaring the war at an end. Wilson vetoed the measure, which was not passed again until July 2, 1921. By that time Wilson was no longer President.

Wilson attempted to make the 1920 presidential election a "solemn referendum" for the League. There is even evidence that, ill as he was, he wanted a third-term nomination. But as the enfeebled Chief Executive sat on the side lines, the Democratic nominee, James M. Cox of Ohio, tirelessly thumped for the League—and went down to defeat at the hands of Warren G. Harding.

On March 4, 1921—Harding's Inauguration Day—police screened off photographers as Wilson was all but bodily lifted into the car that would take him and the President-elect to the Capitol. There, in the President's room, as the clock ticked away the last minutes of his term, he signed a few final bills. At last a committee from both houses of Congress arrived to ask permission to adjourn; its chairman was Henry Cabot Lodge. The two embittered opponents—Wilson throughout had blamed the Massachusetts Republican for singlehandedly defeating the League—addressed one another in frigid, formal phrases.

Former President and Mrs. Wilson did not stay for Harding's Inaugural Address, but left the Capitol by a side door and went immediately to the house on S Street in Washington's Northwest section that they had purchased for their retirement. Woodrow Wilson lived out the remaining three years of his life in semiseclusion. At first a guard had been hired, but there were no crowds of curious people to be restrained and he was dismissed.

In early 1924 word leaked out of the quiet house that Wilson was dying. Crowds once more gathered as famous people came to leave their cards. At 11:15 A.M. on February 3 Wilson died; his last word had been "Edith."

Calvin Coolidge—President since Harding's death the preceding summer—attended the small private funeral at the S Street house, but Senator Lodge, named to a committee to represent Congress, was excluded at Mrs. Wilson's request. Colonel House was not invited.

For the next four decades, Edith Wilson kept alive the memory of her husband, her increasingly infrequent appearances in public always eliciting the comment: "Is she still living?" She died in October, 1961, on the day she was scheduled to appear at the dedication of the Woodrow Wilson Bridge, which crosses the Potomac.

—JOSEPH L. GARDNER

Woodrow Wilson

A PICTURE PORTFOLIO

In 1919, after Wilson had sacrificed his health to crusade for peace and American participation in the League of Nations, he was awarded the Nobel Peace Prize.

Woodrow Wilson campaigned vigorously in the 1912 election, stumping the country from the rear platform of a train (above). His easy humor pleased the crowds, who gathered in railroad yards and on top of boxcars to hear him. "Fellow citizens and gentlemen in the pit, and ladies and gentlemen in the boxes," he began at one whistle-stop. The voters liked the candidate's lucid arguments for the New Freedom and his pledge of economic emancipation through tariff, trust, and banking reform.

A former college professor, Wilson (looking fragile and scholarly on the 1912 campaign button at right) had to overcome the stigma of the egghead. But his unaffected manner soon won the confidence of the voters. "Give it to 'em, Doc," yelled out one small-town farmer during one of Wilson's speeches, "you're all right."

WIN WITH WILSON

"PRESIDENT OF ALL
THE PEOPLE"

Woodrow Wilson led the Democrats to victory in 1912 as a new force in the progressive movement. Former president of Princeton University and governor of New Jersey, he was neither as conservative as his Republican opponent, William Howard Taft, nor as radical as the impulsive Theodore Roosevelt, candidate of the third-party Progressives. Rational and articulate, Wilson presented an intelligent, liberal program that he heralded as the New Freedom. His was, however, a somewhat limited progressivism, stressing economic rather than social reforms; Wilson did not approve of direct social legislation. He attacked former President Roosevelt's proposed minimum-wage program as paternalistic and dismissed the problem of woman suffrage as "not a question that is dealt with by the National Government at all." One of Wilson's concerns was winning the votes of immigrant groups. Ten years earlier he had published a conservative *History of the American People*, in which he had deplored the new wave of immigration. While he had since altered his position, Italian-, Hungarian-, and Polish-born voters could not easily forget a passage in the *History* referring to them as "the more sordid and hapless elements of their population. . . ." The Negroes were another minority group that posed a problem. Although the Democratic managers did not wish to alienate Negro voters in the North, they were determined to preserve the Solid South, even if it meant, as a party spokesman declared in an unfortunate editorial, "the subjection of the negro, politically. . . ." Yet there is little doubt that Wilson himself had profound concern for social justice. And the results of the election seemed to indicate that most Americans were convinced, as a Negro editor put it, that Wilson would be "President of all the people of every section, and of every race."

The 1912 campaign became a three-way race for the Presidency when Theodore Roosevelt, declaring himself "as strong as a bull moose," bolted the Republican party to head the new Progressive ticket. The Clifford Berryman cartoon above shows the three candidates, Wilson, Taft, and Roosevelt, starting off on the rough road that would lead one of them to the White House. Roosevelt's Bull Moose hampered the progress of the conservative Republican candidate, and Taft soon dropped behind. The race became a contest between Roosevelt and Wilson, whose progressive platforms seemed to be very similar. (Editor William Allen White likened the difference to "that fantastic imaginary gulf that always has existed between tweedle-dum and tweedle-dee.")

JOY AND SADNESS

After all the official ceremonies of Inauguration Day, 1913, the Wilson family was finally left alone with a few personal friends. Happily they set out to explore the Executive Mansion. "There was a continual running through the house from one room to another," an observer recalled, "a shrill voice screaming to someone else as a new place was discovered." The President, his wife, Ellen, and their three daughters were delighted with their new quarters. Mrs. Wilson converted the upstairs Oval Room into a family haven of books and paintings. But the harmony was shattered by Ellen's death the next summer. "I never understood before what a broken heart meant," the President told a friend.

EUROPEAN PICTURES

The Wilson girls shared a love for music, dance, and theater. In a 1913 benefit performance of the Bird Masque, *vivacious Eleanor Wilson (above) danced the part of Ornis, the Bird Spirit. Her older sister Margaret provided the voice in the background.*

The First Lady serves tea to her three daughters, Margaret, Eleanor, and Jessie, in a 1913 oil by Robert Vonnah (right). Ellen Wilson was a creative woman with a talent for painting, but her easel was put aside while she worked tirelessly to help eliminate the squalid slums in the District of Columbia.

Wilson's two youngest daughters were married in the White House within six months of each other; Jessie (with wedding party above) to Francis B. Sayre and Eleanor to her father's Secretary of the Treasury, William G. McAdoo. The eldest daughter, Margaret (below with her "graphanola"), seemed to be content with a more contemplative life.

747

UPS AND DOWNS

Wilson's first term was a triumph for his economic program. Import duties were lowered by the Underwood Tariff (containing a provision for the new federal income tax), banking and currency control were centralized under the Federal Reserve System, and monopolies were further restricted by the Federal Trade Commission and Clayton Antitrust acts. The President's foreign policy, however, was less successful, involving the United States in the chaotic Mexican Revolution. Shortly before Wilson's inauguration, Mexico's democratic revolutionary leader had been assassinated and a reactionary dictatorship had been established under General Victoriano Huerta. Refusing to recognize the oppressive regime, Wilson began to exert pressure to remove Huerta. Although Wilson's actions undoubtedly grew out of a belief in the virtues of democracy and the evils of dictatorship, his interference angered not only Huerta but the Mexicans as well. When an incident involving the arrest of American citizens provided an excuse for armed United States intervention at Veracruz in 1914, the Mexicans united behind the dictator. The dispute was arbitrated, Huerta resigned, and the Americans withdrew—but seeds of resentment had been planted.

Wilson sits with members of his first Cabinet, above. They are (left to right) Secretary of the Treasury William McAdoo, Attorney General James McReynolds, Secretary of the Navy Josephus Daniels, and Secretary of State William J. Bryan. Bryan resigned when American involvement in World War I seemed to be imminent.

Wilson's Latin-American policies were often moralistic and didactic. "I am going to teach the South American republics to elect good men!" he once told a British diplomat. In a 1913 cartoon from London's Punch magazine (left), Wilson wags his finger at Mexico in obvious disapproval of the course of the Mexican Revolution. America's interference in its neighbor's affairs created deep, lasting resentments in Mexico.

In the "Woodrow and the Bean-Stalk" cartoon below, Wilson chops the tangled roots of high protection and fells the giant representing monopoly. Wilson's downward revision of the tariff was part of a larger program of economic reform designed to check the power of the trusts, revitalize competition among smaller businesses, and bolster the United States economy in general.

MEN WITH NEW IDEAS

BOTH: CULVER PICTURES

THORSTEIN VEBLEN

Thorstein Veblen died in August, 1929, a few months before the stock market collapse that seemed to vindicate the economic theories he had been advancing for years. Veblen's youth in a clannish Norwegian farm community in Minnesota left him with a distrust of business and with a defensive uneasiness about the outside world. In his first book, *The Theory of the Leisure Class*, published in 1899 while he was teaching at the University of Chicago, he wrote that the nation's economy was based on prices dangerously inflated by social dictates rather than on the value of goods. (Veblen coined the phrase "conspicuous consumption.") *The Theory of Business Enterprise*, published in 1904, and subsequent writings savagely condemned allegiance to the profit motive and scored the influence of business on law, politics, and education. Veblen deplored monopolistic control of production and in his later works suggested that a hierarchy of technicians should oversee the country's commerce. Revolutionary as his ideas were—and labyrinthine as his prose was—Thorstein Veblen was an influential force in the trend toward tighter government control of private enterprise. He taught at Stanford University in California, the University of Missouri in Columbia, and the New School for Social Research in New York City.

JOHN DEWEY

The American philosopher John Dewey was as practical as he was idealistic, a doer as well as a thinker. Born in Vermont in 1859, he received his doctorate from Johns Hopkins in 1884. As an activist he was attracted by the writings of William James, who was popularizing the philosophical dogma called pragmatism as formulated by Charles Sanders Peirce. Regarding the world through Darwinian eyes, the pragmatists said that truth, like the earth itself, was ever-changing, evolving, and variable; they believed in intellectual flexibility. Dewey synthesized his pragmatic philosophy in the simple slogan "learning by doing," which he applied to his experiments at the Laboratory School of the University of Chicago around the turn of the century. The results of these experiments have profoundly influenced American education. The pragmatic belief that philosophy had to deal not just with abstractions but with social and legal realities kept Dewey busy on and off campus during his years (1904–1930) at Columbia University in New York. A frequent champion of unpopular causes—he opposed, for example, the Sacco-Vanzetti executions in 1927—he was a founder of the American Civil Liberties Union. Although he retired from teaching, he was a lecturer and political activist until he died in 1952.

FRANK LLOYD WRIGHT

"A sense of the organic is indispensable to an architect," wrote Frank Lloyd Wright. A student of Louis H. Sullivan (with whom he worked in Chicago from 1887 to 1893), he gratefully acknowledged his debt to the master's basic premise, "form follows function." Working independently after 1893, Wright concentrated on the private dwelling, evolving his own indigenous style in his so-called prairie houses. Integrating form with the needs of modern man, his structures harmonize with the surrounding landscape to achieve a unified, organic whole. Notable among his designs are his Wisconsin summer home, Taliesin East; the Coonley, Willitts, and Robie houses in Illinois; the Barnsdall house in California; the Jones house in Oklahoma; the Kaufmann house in Pennsylvania; and many other private residences. Slow to win acceptance in the United States, Wright was an immediate success abroad. His Imperial Hotel in Tokyo was an architectural masterpiece that survived the earthquake of 1923. Two of his most impressive nonresidential structures are the Johnson Wax Building in Wisconsin and the Solomon R. Guggenheim Museum in New York, which was completed shortly after his death in 1959. Taliesin West in Arizona served as Wright's winter home, studio, and school for young architects.

DAVID WARK GRIFFITH

"Father of the film art" and "king of directors," David Wark Griffith revolutionized the motion-picture industry. Close-ups, long shots, mist photography, backlighting, the fade-out and fade-in, and the moving camera were but a few of his pioneering techniques. Born in 1875, Griffith began his career as an actor, became an assistant director with the Biograph Company in 1908, and that year directed his first film, *The Adventures of Dollie*. A few years later he made the first American four-reeler, *Judith of Bethulia*, and in 1914 he produced the famous and controversial *The Birth of a Nation*. Based on *The Clansman*, a novel that was prejudicially sympathetic to the Reconstruction South, the epic aroused angry passions in the North and helped to revive the infamous Ku Klux Klan in the South. It was a phenomenal box-office success. Griffith went on to produce *Intolerance* (1916), *Broken Blossoms* (1919), *Way Down East* (1920), *Orphans of the Storm* (1922), and *America* (1924). He introduced and developed such performers as Mary Pickford and Lillian Gish and was a founder of the United Artists Corporation. Because he spent huge sums in his efforts to make original films, Griffith became anathema in Hollywood, where profits were more important than artistic achievement. He died in 1948.

CULVER PICTURES

Despite Germany's warning (above), Americans were stunned by the Lusitania *sinking.*

AVOIDING WAR

Wilson's problems with Mexico were not over. In January, 1916, a Mexican chieftain called Pancho Villa began a vindictive campaign that culminated in a bloody raid on Columbus, New Mexico. Wilson ordered a punitive expedition against Villa, who lured the gringos deep into Mexico. Alarmed by American penetration, the Mexican government called out its own forces, and all-out war was narrowly avoided when Wilson withdrew the troops. Meanwhile, the United States was trying to avoid becoming involved in a conflict of far greater proportion, the one then raging in Europe. Issuing a neutrality proclamation, the President asked Americans to be "impartial in thought as well as in action." But Germany's violations of neutral rights and the *Lusitania* sinking strained neutrality almost to the breaking point.

A punitive expedition against the bloodthirsty Mexican bandit Pancho Villa in 1916 gave the United States an opportunity to test combat planes like the Curtiss model above, later used in World War I.

As America headed toward war, pacifist delegations such as the one below stepped up their pleas for peace.

*Gossips had a heyday as the President began courting Edith Galt.
The couple slowed down wagging tongues by getting married in
December, 1915. (Above is a newspaper illustration celebrating
the match.) On one occasion Wilson had sent orchids to Mrs. Galt
with this charming note: "You are the only woman I know who can
wear an orchid. Generally it's the orchid that wears the woman."*

The button (left) and truck (below) urged Wilson's re-election.

A SHORT-LIVED PEACE

As the threat of war increased, the nation was faced with the 1916 presidential election. Opposing Republican Charles Evans Hughes, Wilson and his Democratic managers based their campaign on the issues of progressivism and peace. Having recently signed reform measures implementing farm credit, federal workmen's compensation, restriction of child labor, and an eight-hour day for railroad workers, Wilson's record was stronger than ever. He had reversed his 1912 position on social-welfare legislation and had adopted a progressive platform that one independent supporter described as "national in scope, liberal in purpose, and effective in action." But Americans were less concerned with domestic issues than with the uncertainties of the war in Europe. Sensing the overwhelming desire of the average citizen to stay out of the conflict, the Democrats effectively pointed out that "our country is at peace in a world at war." Wilson's victory owed much to the fact that he had, somehow, managed to keep the country neutral. Knowing how easily that neutrality could be destroyed, the President made a last noble plea for peace in January, 1917. Calling for freedom of the seas, disarmament, and government by consent of the people, he appealed to the belligerents for "peace without victory." His plea fell on deaf ears; in February Germany resumed unrestricted submarine warfare. No longer able to resist "the irresistible logic of events," the United States, on April 6, 1917, declared war on Kaiser Wilhelm's Germany.

CHARLES EVANS HUGHES

Charles Evans Hughes was perhaps the only candidate capable of wooing the Progressives back into the Republican fold in 1916. An associate justice of the Supreme Court and a former governor of New York, he was remembered by Progressives for reforming state government, whereas Republicans liked his conservative record on the Court. A graduate of Brown University, Hughes received his law degree from Columbia in 1884. Practicing in New York City, he distinguished himself as counsel for the prosecution in a number of cases involving abuses by public utilities and life insurance companies. He served as New York's liberal governor from 1906 until 1910, when his Supreme Court appointment removed him from the political fray that split the Progressives from the regular Republicans two years later. Nominated by the Republicans in 1916, he was supported by the Progressives after Theodore Roosevelt refused their nomination; Roosevelt reluctantly endorsed the bewhiskered Hughes, whom he once dubbed the "bearded lady." Narrowly defeated by Wilson, Hughes returned to law. He served as Secretary of State from 1921 to 1926, became a member of the Permanent Court of Arbitration in 1926, and in 1930 was appointed a judge on the Permanent Court of International Justice. That same year he was named Chief Justice of the Supreme Court. He served in that post until 1941.

WAGING WAR

Merica had to wage the war she had declared, and Wilson's gargantuan task was to overcome the nation's peacetime mentality and the unpreparedness of its industrial machine. Trench warfare soon stripped the fighting of its glamour, and it was not easy to make conscription palatable to Americans. The War Industries Board, headed by Bernard Baruch, had almost dictatorial control over the country's commerce, but did not abuse it; the wartime administration was free of corruption. Some programs—notably shipbuilding—never really got rolling, but the nation went along with "Wheatless Mondays" and "Meatless Tuesdays." Britain got her food, and France eventually got her men—more than two million of them. A barrage of Wilsonian propaganda pamphlets eroded German morale; even General Erich Ludendorff, still blind to other defeats, later admitted that "Germany failed in the fight of intellects."

Posters such as the one above urged American men to rally to the defense of their country in 1917.

Etched against the stubble of once-wooded French terrain, Americans of the Second Division's 23rd Infantry (above) keep low to avoid German fire. Among the Americans stationed in Europe during World War I were Douglas MacArthur, George C. Marshall, George S. Patton, Fiorello La Guardia, and Harry S. Truman.

FIGHTING AMERICANS

CULVER PICTURES

NATIONAL ARCHIVES

ALVIN C. YORK

Alvin C. York, a thirty-year-old sergeant from Tennessee, displayed such great bravery in 1918 that his name became an international synonym for heroism. York was a member of the American First Army, which had been assigned the thankless task of ousting the Germans from the Argonne Forest just west of the Meuse River. The Yanks were fighting a canny enemy in rugged, dreary terrain; the going was slow and confusion reigned. On October 8 York led a detachment that suffered heavy losses while forcing the surrender of a group of Germans. When a sudden machine-gun burst killed most of York's companions, he dropped to one knee, wiped out the machine-gun nest with rifle fire, and then shot the Germans who charged him. In all, he killed twenty enemy soldiers. Coolly marching his prisoners ahead of him, Sergeant York captured a second machine-gun emplacement. He took a total of one hundred and thirty-two prisoners and captured thirty-five machine guns. Marshal Ferdinand Foch called it the greatest achievement by any noncommissioned officer in the war, and General Pershing officially cited York's valor. York, who was awarded the Congressional Medal of Honor and the French *Croix de guerre*, was portrayed by Gary Cooper in the prizewinning 1941 motion picture *Sergeant York*.

WILLIAM L. MITCHELL

Billy Mitchell, thwarted in his attempts to convince officials of the future importance of aviation, was vindicated only after his death. Mitchell enlisted in the Army in 1898. He served in Cuba, the Philippines, and Alaska and in 1912, at thirty-two, became the youngest member of the General Staff. Aware of the airplane's great military potential, he helped form the American Expeditionary Forces Aviation Program in 1917. The following year Mitchell led 1,481 Allied aircraft in World War I's primary air effort, the assault on the Saint-Mihiel salient. As assistant chief of air service after the war, Mitchell advocated a separate air force, but was frustrated by conservative military leaders. He felt the airplane had made the battleship obsolete and proved his point by bombing target ships off the Virginia coast. The Navy and War departments remained obdurate, however, and after two naval air accidents in September of 1925, Mitchell accused them of "criminal negligence." He was court-martialed and suspended from duty in 1926. Mitchell continued to stress the need for air superiority and warned that American defenses were inadequate. The Army Air Corps was created in 1926, but he still lamented the tardiness of official action. He was awarded a posthumous Medal of Honor in 1946.

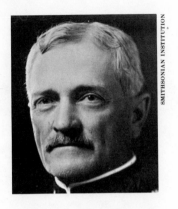

JOHN J. PERSHING

'General Pershing is the stubbornest man I know," said Georges Clemenceau, "and I am saying that knowing Mr. Wilson. . . ." An obstinate man himself, Clemenceau knew whereof he spoke. When John J. Pershing led the American Expeditionary Forces to France in 1917, he insisted that it be an independent army (otherwise, he felt, American morale would suffer), and he resisted many of the repeated attempts to use his men as reinforcements. The A.E.F.'s first battle as the American First Army was at Saint-Mihiel in September of 1918, and Pershing's 1,200,000 doughboys followed that victory with the Meuse-Argonne campaign, which brought Germany to its knees. An 1886 graduate of West Point, Pershing fought Indians in the West and served in Cuba during the Spanish-American War and in the Philippines later. He was made a brigadier general in 1906. The deaths of his wife and three daughters in a fire in 1915, and the frustratingly futile pursuit of Pancho Villa in Mexico the following year, left their marks on Pershing: more than ever the stern disciplinarian deserved his sobriquet Black Jack. In 1919 Pershing was made general of the armies, a position previously held only by George Washington. His *My Experiences in the World War* won a Pulitzer Prize in 1932. General Pershing died in July, 1948.

EDWARD V. RICKENBACKER

Edward V. Rickenbacker, unable to apply for Army flying school because, at twenty-six, he was considered too old, went to France as a chauffeur on General Pershing's staff. There, in 1917, he convinced Billy Mitchell to approve him for aerial training, and he eventually became the top American pilot of World War I. Between early 1918 and the armistice, he shot down twenty-two German planes and four observation balloons; his total would undoubtedly have been higher had not an ear infection grounded him for two months. Captain Rickenbacker received the *Croix de guerre* and the Congressional Medal of Honor. Always drawn to machines that combined speed and danger, Eddie Rickenbacker had been a professional racing driver from 1911 to 1917. An auto company of his own failed in 1925, and after a series of jobs in aviation he engineered the purchase of Eastern Air Lines in 1938. He was that company's president until 1953 and chairman of its board until he retired in 1963. During World War II Rickenbacker flew special noncombat missions that took him from Iceland to Australia. In October of 1942 his plane was forced down in the South Pacific; twenty-three days on a life raft inspired his book, *Seven Came Through*, published in 1943. His World War I experiences are recorded in his *Fighting the Flying Circus*.

DISAPPOINTMENT

"What I seem to see—I hope I am wrong—is a tragedy of disappointment." The speaker was Woodrow Wilson, on his way to the Paris peace conference, but it was an uncharacteristic remark. Despite recent off-year election embarrassments, Wilson still felt that he and his Fourteen Points would make the world "fit and safe to live in." His anxieties were fleeting, for Europe welcomed him as a messiah, convincing him that there was, after all, hope for implementing his program. But, as historian John Garraty wrote, Wilson's "combination of altruism, idealism and power was his undoing, for it intensified his tendency to be overbearing and undermined his judgment." Wilson did not understand the aims and bartering tactics of his colleagues in Paris. Remarked Lloyd George—who had just made political hay at home on a "Make Germany pay" platform—"If you want to succeed in politics, you must keep your conscience well under control." Caring only for France, Georges Clemenceau said, "Mr. Wilson bores me with his Fourteen Points; why, God Almighty has only ten!" The Allies, with their secret treaties and their eye-for-an-eye attitude toward Germany, tended to regard the points as a *ruse de guerre* that had made the enemy surrender but bound the victors no longer. Wilson permitted a number of his points to be modified, but insisted that any treaty provide for a league of nations—a league that would compensate for the compromises he was making along the way. The Allies, with Wilson's concessions in hand, were willing; but at home the President found that the package deal was unpopular, and his own attitude ("The Senate must take its medicine") only calcified the opposition. Weary in body and mind, Wilson wanted to take his cause to the people. "I know I am at the end of my tether," he said, but "the trip is necessary to save the Treaty. . . . No decent man can count his own personal fortunes."

Between his arrival in Europe and the opening of the peace conference, Wilson visited Italy and England. In London he received the gold chest shown above, containing portraits of himself and King George. Wilson did not tour any former combat areas, and some Army personnel chafed at the thought of his ocean liner riding at anchor while they could not go stateside for lack of transportation. But the soldiers shown left, above, took jubilant exception to "Hindenburg Strasse" in a French town and renamed it for their President. Wilson was cheered everywhere he went in those hopeful, preconference days, and the extent of his influence was reflected in a standing joke among American newsmen working in Rome. Two Italian laborers, the story went, met on the street. One said that the Pope was ailing; the other replied, "Ah, that is too bad, I hope he doesn't die . . . for el Presidente Wilson might appoint a Protestant." The Big Four are shown at left during the peace talks. Lloyd George, far left, listens to Italy's Vittorio Orlando make a point; President Wilson stands with Georges Clemenceau of France, possessor of a magnificent walrus mustache.

Wilson is shown above in San Francisco in 1919, a few days before he was stricken. Senators Hiram Johnson, James Reed, and William Borah, opposed to the treaty, followed Wilson's itinerary and delivered anti-League speeches to the same audiences the President had addressed. The defeat of the League of Nations inspired innumerable cartoons, such as the one below, entitled "Grasping at Straws," from the San Francisco Chronicle.

"WE SHALL PREVAIL"

Can you come to me, Edith?" called Woodrow Wilson from the next compartment, "I'm terribly sick." Aboard the presidential train in the early hours of September 26, 1919, the tour in defense of the League of Nations came to an abrupt halt. Wilson indeed was ill: this stroke was followed by another a week later, and White House physician Cary Grayson was convinced that there had been serious brain damage. For more than half a year the world knew little about the President of the United States. Edith, Grayson, and Joe Tumulty, Wilson's secretary, sheltered him with astonishing success, keeping the extent of his disability the strictest of secrets. Wilson remained adamant that the League be accepted without reservations ("Let Lodge compromise!") and eventually saw all hope for American participation in the League— and the treaty—evaporate. Wilson grew testy; at times he brooded; there were periodic lapses of memory and unpredictable crying spells; he doted on the movies that were shown at the White House two or three times a week. On April 13, 1920, he held his first Cabinet meeting in months. Secretary of Agriculture David Houston said the President "looked old, worn and haggard; it was enough to make one weep." When the Wilsons vacated the White House and moved to S Street in 1921, the former President's life became quiet and routine. He moved about with the help of an elevator and the ever-present cane; Grayson allowed him one visitor a day, for half an hour; Edith screened the mail, played Canfield with him, read him to sleep. Still, the fire smoldered. To an Armistice Day crowd, gathered in front of the house three months before he died, Woodrow Wilson said, in a firm voice, "I have seen fools resist Providence before and I have seen their destruction, and it will come upon these again, utter destruction and contempt; that we shall prevail is as sure as that God reigns."

HARRIS & EWING

Woodrow Wilson steadies himself, above, for what would be one of his last photographs. His strokes had paralyzed his left side. While recovering he took pains to show only his right profile in public and kept his useless left hand out of sight.

FACTS IN SUMMARY: WOODROW WILSON

CHRONOLOGY

UNITED STATES		WILSON
Buchanan elected President	1856	*Born December 28*
Lincoln elected President	1860	
Civil War begins	1861	
Battle of Gettysburg	1863	
Lee surrenders at Appomattox	1865	
Lincoln assassinated		
Andrew Johnson impeached	1868	
Grant elected President		
Bank panic	1873	*Enters Davidson College*
	1875	*Enters Princeton*
Hayes elected President	1877	
	1879	*Studies at University of Virginia Law School*
Garfield elected President	1880	
	1882	*Admitted to the bar*
Pendleton Act	1883	*Studies at Johns Hopkins University*
Cleveland elected President	1884	
	1885	*Publishes* Congressional Government
		Marries Ellen Axson
		Teaches at Bryn Mawr
	1886	*Receives Ph.D. from Johns Hopkins*
Harrison elected President	1888	*Teaches at Wesleyan*
Sherman Antitrust Act	1890	*Appointed professor at Princeton*
Cleveland re-elected President	1892	
McKinley elected President	1896	
Spanish-American War	1898	
Theodore Roosevelt becomes President	1901	
Northern Securities case	1902	*Named president of Princeton*
Taft elected President	1908	
Mann-Elkins Act	1910	*Elected governor of New Jersey*
	1912	*Elected President*
Sixteenth Amendment	1913	*Asks Congress to lower tariffs*
Seventeenth Amendment		*Proposes Federal Reserve Act*
Underwood Tariff		
Federal Reserve Act		

UNITED STATES		WILSON
World War I begins	1914	*Orders troops to occupy Veracruz*
Federal Trade Commission Act		*Urges establishment of Federal Trade Commission*
Clayton Antitrust Act		
		Ellen Wilson dies
Lusitania sunk	1915	*Warns Germany against attacks on neutral ships*
		Marries Edith Galt
		Orders troops to intervene in Haitian revolt
National Defense Act	1916	*Sends troops to Mexican border*
Federal Farm Loan Act		
Denmark cedes Virgin Islands to U.S.		*Re-elected President*
		Asks belligerents in Europe to state war aims
Germany resumes unrestricted submarine warfare	1917	*Severs diplomatic relations with Germany*
War with Germany declared		*Asks Congress to declare war on Germany*
Liberty Loan Act		*Establishes War Industries Board*
Selective Service Act		*Places railroads under federal control*
Espionage Act		
Congress adopts prohibition amendment		
Sedition Act	1918	*Issues Fourteen Points*
Belleau Wood		*Appoints National War Labor Board*
Second Battle of the Marne		*Sails to France to attend peace conference*
Meuse-Argonne Offensive		
War ends November 11		
Eighteenth Amendment ratified	1919	*Helps draft Treaty of Versailles and League of Nations Covenant*
Senate rejects League of Nations		*Tours country on behalf of League of Nations*
		Incapacitated by stroke
		Awarded Nobel Peace Prize
Nineteenth Amendment ratified	1920	
Harding elected President		
	1921	*Retires to private life*
Coolidge becomes President	1923	
	1924	*Dies February 3*

BIOGRAPHICAL FACTS

BIRTH: Staunton, Va., Dec. 28, 1856
ANCESTRY: Scotch-Irish
FATHER: Joseph Ruggles Wilson; b. Steubenville, Oh⸱
Feb. 28, 1822; d. Princeton, N.J., Jan. 21, 1903

THER'S OCCUPATION: Presbyterian minister

OTHER: Jessie Woodrow Wilson; b. Carlisle, England,
6; d. Clarksville, Tenn., April 15, 1888

STERS: Marion (1850–1890); Annie Josephine (1854–
6)

OTHER: Joseph (1866–?)

RST WIFE: Ellen Louise Axson; b. Rome, Ga., May
1860; d. Washington, D.C., Aug. 6, 1914

RST MARRIAGE: Savannah, Ga., June 24, 1885

COND WIFE: Edith Bolling Galt; b. Wytheville, Va.,
t. 15, 1872; d. Dec. 28, 1961

COND MARRIAGE: Washington, D.C., Dec. 18, 1915

ILDREN: Margaret Woodrow (1886–1944); Jessie
odrow (1887–1932); Eleanor Randolph (1889–1967)

UCATION: Private tutors; Davidson College; Prince-
University; University of Virginia Law School; Johns
pkins University

LIGIOUS AFFILIATION: Presbyterian

ME: Woodrow Wilson House, 2340 S Street, N.W.,
shington, D.C.

CUPATIONS BEFORE PRESIDENCY: Lawyer;
cher; college president

E-PRESIDENTIAL OFFICE: Governor of New
sey

LITICAL PARTY: Democratic

ATH: Washington, D.C., Feb. 3, 1924

ACE OF BURIAL: Washington Cathedral, Washing-
, D.C.

ECTION OF 1912

CANDIDATES	ELECTORAL VOTE	POPULAR VOTE
Woodrow Wilson Democratic	435	6,296,547
Theodore Roosevelt Progressive	88	4,118,571
William H. Taft Republican	8	3,486,720
Eugene V. Debs Socialist	—	900,672
Eugene W. Chafin Prohibition	—	206,275

RST ADMINISTRATION

AUGURATION: March 4, 1913; the Capitol, Washing-
n, D.C.

CE PRESIDENT: Thomas R. Marshall

CRETARY OF STATE: William Jennings Bryan;
obert Lansing (from June 23, 1915)

CRETARY OF THE TREASURY: William G.
cAdoo

CRETARY OF WAR: Lindley M. Garrison; Newton
. Baker (from March 9, 1916)

TTORNEY GENERAL: James C. McReynolds; Thomas
. Gregory (from Sept. 3, 1914)

POSTMASTER GENERAL: Albert S. Burleson

SECRETARY OF THE NAVY: Josephus Daniels

SECRETARY OF THE INTERIOR: Franklin K. Lane

SECRETARY OF AGRICULTURE: David F. Houston

SECRETARY OF COMMERCE: William C. Redfield

SECRETARY OF LABOR: William B. Wilson

SUPREME COURT APPOINTMENTS: James C.
McReynolds (1914); Louis D. Brandeis (1916); John H.
Clarke (1916)

63rd CONGRESS (March 4, 1913–March 4, 1915):
Senate: 51 Democrats; 44 Republicans; 1 Other
House: 291 Democrats; 127 Republicans; 17 Others
64th CONGRESS (March 4, 1915–March 4, 1917):
Senate: 56 Democrats; 40 Republicans
House: 230 Democrats; 196 Republicans; 9 Others

END OF PRESIDENTIAL TERM: March 4, 1917

ELECTION OF 1916

CANDIDATES	ELECTORAL VOTE	POPULAR VOTE
Woodrow Wilson Democratic	277	9,127,695
Charles E. Hughes Republican	254	8,533,507
A. L. Benson Socialist	—	585,113
J. Frank Hanly Prohibition	—	220,506

SECOND ADMINISTRATION

INAUGURATION: March 5, 1917; the Capitol, Washington, D.C.

VICE PRESIDENT: Thomas R. Marshall

SECRETARY OF STATE: Robert Lansing; Bainbridge
Colby (from March 23, 1920)

SECRETARY OF THE TREASURY: William G.
McAdoo; Carter Glass (from Dec. 16, 1918); David F.
Houston (from Feb. 2, 1920)

SECRETARY OF WAR: Newton D. Baker

ATTORNEY GENERAL: Thomas W. Gregory; A.
Mitchell Palmer (from March 5, 1919)

POSTMASTER GENERAL: Albert S. Burleson

SECRETARY OF THE NAVY: Josephus Daniels

SECRETARY OF THE INTERIOR: Franklin K. Lane;
John B. Payne (from March 13, 1920)

SECRETARY OF AGRICULTURE: David F. Houston;
Edwin T. Meredith (from Feb. 2, 1920)

SECRETARY OF COMMERCE: William C. Redfield;
Joshua W. Alexander (from Dec. 16, 1919)

SECRETARY OF LABOR: William B. Wilson

65th CONGRESS (March 4, 1917–March 4, 1919):
Senate: 53 Democrats; 42 Republicans
House: 216 Democrats; 210 Republicans; 6 Others
66th CONGRESS (March 4, 1919–March 4, 1921):
Senate: 49 Republicans; 47 Democrats
House: 240 Republicans; 190 Democrats; 3 Others

END OF PRESIDENTIAL TERM: March 4, 1921

WARREN GAMALIEL HARDING

Will Rogers called it the "great morality panic of 1924." Stirred by rumors of corruption in the Harding administration and further stirred, no doubt, by the fact that 1924 was an election year, Congress had decided to do some investigating. The resulting panic was a two-way affair: certainly the haste of the potential accused to find an inconspicuous niche somewhere was no madder than the dash of the opportunists anxious to act as accusers. The press and public, however, seemed to enjoy the investigations and to enjoy watching the politicians go at one another with lynch-mob vindictiveness.

The rumors were well-founded—truer, probably, than their mongers had known. First there was Secretary of the Interior Albert B. Fall, who had leased two government oil deposits—the Teapot Dome reserve in Wyoming and the Elk Hills fields in California—to private interests from which he had received at least one hundred and twenty-five thousand dollars in personal "loans." Then there were Harding's Veterans Bureau chief and alien property custodian, who were denounced (and eventually imprisoned, as was Fall) for defrauding the government by awarding—or, more accurately, selling—contracts to whoever gave them the largest kickback. And, to make matters worse, there was Attorney General Harry M. Daugherty, who, it was discovered, had known all about the corruption, but had not prosecuted the corrupt nor even tried to stop them. Indeed, he was too busy with his own very profitable business: collecting graft from prohibition violators. There were big men involved, and little men, oil millionaires and bureaucrats—all infecting the United States government with a malignancy not easily removed.

The Teapot Dome scandal was the most spectacular and notorious of all, for it revealed how thoroughly corruption had penetrated the Harding ad-

This portrait now hangs in the Harding Museum in Marion, Ohio.

ministration. The President had surrounded himself with his old political cronies. He had made them his government and he trusted them. As a result, the executive branch was a tightly assembled, smooth-running machine. Chief Executive, Cabinet members, department heads—all knew and liked each other, worked well together, and gladly approved whatever one of them wanted approved. In one instance Fall suggested that the oil reserves for which Navy Secretary Edwin Denby was responsible be transferred to the Department of the Interior. Harding and Denby had no objection; the President signed and Fall leased. Everything was properly signed and filed. Even after the scandal broke, it took the government three years to legally invalidate the Teapot Dome and Elk Hills leases.

Mercifully, Warren Gamaliel Harding did not have to endure the disgrace of his misplaced trust. He had died on August 2, 1923, a year before the scandals were made public. "Few deaths are unmingled tragedies," wrote biographer Samuel Hopkins Adams. "Harding's was not. He died in time." If he had lived, he would have been brokenhearted, but he probably would have stood by his friends; for Warren Harding, by near-unanimous agreement of historians a very poor President, was a very good friend.

Harding, the oldest of eight children, was born on November 2, 1865, in Blooming Grove, Ohio. His father was a farmer, horse trader, and casual speculator with a talent for veterinary work and an abiding interest in medicine. In fact, when Warren was eight years old, George Harding went off to medical school and returned home a physician.

But it was one of George Harding's speculative investments that had the greatest impact on his son. Two years earlier, the elder Harding had bought an interest in a regional newspaper, and the six-year-old Warren was allowed to be the printer's errand boy. Young as he was, he was significantly affected by his brief exposure to the newspaper business.

Later in his career, Warren Harding would reminisce fondly about his rural up-

Warren Harding was a sixteen-year-old school-teacher when he posed for this photograph in 1882.

bringing. The truth was, however, that he did not like farm chores; Harding preferred the life in town. Although he was not much of a scholar, his mother hoped he might become a preacher and in 1879 sent him to Ohio Central College. He was not interested in the ministry and apparently was not sure what he wanted to do with his life, but he did enjoy the school. He was an althorn player in the band, an occasional debater, and editor of the yearbook. During vacations he took what employment he could find: he worked in a sawmill, as a broom-maker, and as a railroad construction laborer.

But manual labor was easy compared to teaching school, which he did after his graduation in 1882. "It was the hardest job I ever had," he recalled, and he resigned after one term, joining his family in the town of Marion, where his father had moved in search of a greener practice. There Harding studied law for a while, but did not like it and quit; he tried selling insurance, but did not like that either. He loved Marion, however, and made a reputation as a good leader and capable handler of money by successfully managing the finances of the local base-ball team and of the Citizens' Cornet Band.

His big chance came in 1884. The *Star*, a town newspaper that was failing, was for sale for three hundred dollars and acceptance of its mortgage. Harding talked two friends into a partnership, arguing that Marion's potential growth ensured a sound future. The first several years were gloomy; his friends lost interest, and Harding bought them out. Soon Marion did in fact begin to grow. Although the *Star* did not exactly prosper, it held its own and survived.

"You can read the Marion *Star* for the thirty-odd years that Warren has owned it," George Harding later recalled, "without finding a vilification of anybody in any issue." Harding himself observed in retrospect that "the paper was always on a higher plane than getting even." In truth, Harding, like most small-town newspapermen, could match venom with the best of them and did so regularly. Once, when his chief competitor expressed in print doubt about the sincerity of the *Star*'s Republicanism, Editor Harding published the following comments: "This Crawford . . . foams at the mouth whenever his sordid mind grasps anything

done without his counsel. . . . This sour, disgruntled, and disappointed old ass [is] an imbecile whose fits will make him a paralytic, then his way of spitting venom will end."

Crawford's charge that Harding was a "Republican for revenue only" was only partially true. In the *Star*'s early years the editor had tried to maintain an independent editorial policy, for although the town and state were Republican, Marion County was Democratic. Advertising space for official state notices, however, was purchased only in faithfully Republican newspapers, and Harding, anxious to acquire the additional income, finally announced that the *Star* would thenceforth speak for Republicanism. But revenue was not the whole story: Harding's partisanship had often been revealed in the pages of his paper.

After 1891 everything changed at the *Star*. The changes were effected by Florence Kling De Wolfe, the daughter of a rich Marion real-estate and banking magnate. In that year Harding was twenty-six years old; Florence, a widow with a son, was thirty-one. He was handsome, amicable, pleasant, and passive;

Above is the library of Harding's house in Marion, Ohio. Like the homes of many American Presidents, Harding's has been converted into a memorial library and a museum of the President's papers and personal belongings.

she was plain, lacking in charm, fiercely independent, and aggressive. None of Harding's more trustworthy biographers have found the slightest evidence that the two were in love; not one seems to know exactly why they married. But marry they did. Shortly thereafter, when Harding was feeling ill, his wife appeared at the *Star* office. "I went down there intending to help out for a few days," she remembered, "and remained fourteen years." She organized things. She hired and trained a force of delivery boys (whom she was not above spanking, if necessary). She gave very few raises. (Harding would occasionally give raises behind her back; it did not matter to him how much his employees earned because he usually won half the payroll back from them at poker anyway.) "It was her energy and business sense which made the *Star*," according to one of her newsboys. "Her husband was the front. . . . He was a fine small-town or city booster and wrote editorials telling how Marion, Ohio, had more miles of Berea sandstone sidewalks than any town of its size in the United States. Nay, he ventured to say, in the whole world. This was his best line." The recollecting newsboy was Norman Thomas, the Socialist, who always remained a welcome guest in the Harding home—even after that home was the White House.

In the last decade of the century Warren Harding began to take a more active part in Republican politics. The party was glad to have him: he was a prospering editor; an influential citizen active in church, civic, and business ventures (as the *Star* prospered and its editor's influence increased, he became a board member of several Marion corporations); a good speaker; and a willing campaigner. In 1892 he even agreed to be the Republican sacrificial lamb by running for county auditor, an election he was sure to lose. Defeat came very easily. But by 1898 he was taking politics a little more seriously and chose to run for an office he could, and did, win—state senator. "It was not long," wrote a reporter, "before Harding was the most popular man in the legislature. He had the inestimable gift of never forgetting a

man's face or name. He was a regular he-man . . . a great poker-player, and not at all averse to putting a foot on the brass rail." His genuine charm, friendliness, and enthusiasm made him an ideal conciliator for the faction-ridden Ohio Republican party.

Affability—the factor that made Harding and more than compensated for his lack of political expertise—had always eluded Harry M. Daugherty, a skillful, shrewd machine politician and lobbyist who knew everything about politics except how to win elections. Daugherty had first seen Harding at a Republican rally, and because Harding had looked so statesmanlike, had thought, "Gee, what a President he'd make!" The two men became well acquainted during Warren Harding's tenure in the state legislature, and Daugherty began applying his political skills to advance the career of his new friend. In 1902 he helped Harding win the lieutenant governorship. After one term Harding refused to run again. The Republican party in Ohio was engaged in bitter internal quarrels from which Harding, the conciliator, preferred to remain aloof—especially since the Democrats were enjoying a rare dominance in the state. In 1910 he ran for governor and lost. Two years later, however, President William Howard Taft chose Harding to nominate him for re-election at the Republican National Convention. That same year Harding lost a second bid for the Ohio governorship and was prepared to abandon politics, but his wife and Harry Daugherty pressed him into running for the United States Senate in 1914. Taking full charge of the campaign, Daugherty guided Harding to victory.

Harding, who looked like a President, looked even more like a senator; it was said that he could have worn a toga and gotten away with it. The prestige, the social life, and both the camaraderie and the sparring of the Senate were very precious to him, although he did not care much for the work. He preferred golf course to office, race track to committee room, ball park to Senate chamber, and poker table to almost anything.

Harding was reliably Republican and predictably conservative as a senator, vacillating

The presidential election of 1920 was the first in which women (such as the New Yorkers above) were permitted to vote. Warren Harding's handsomeness undoubtedly caused some ladies to vote for the Republican ticket.

only when the prescribed party posture was at odds with the feelings of his constituency. He voted for whatever was good for business, even supporting legislation allowing private interests to employ public resources. He opposed all regulation of industry, even when wartime security required it. And he distrusted labor: on such issues as the eight-hour day for railroad employees and child-labor restriction he chose not to vote at all.

Senator Harding opposed confirmation of Louis D. Brandeis' appointment to the Supreme Court. On the prohibition amendment, he voted "wet" on the first thirty roll calls, but when he saw that the prohibitionists were going to prevail, switched on the final ballot to "dry." And although he admitted that he thought the law unenforceable, he voted to override Wilson's veto of the Volstead Act. Despite his more or less isolationist posture (it was a party-dictated position; Harding himself was fuzzy on international affairs), he generally supported the President's conduct of the war, though not always his aims. He was, in sum, a United States senator of little distinction. And yet in one significant respect he was unique: Warren Harding was a gentleman, a decent and generous person. He was genuinely loved.

These were the happiest years of Harding's life. He won consistently at poker; he had many good friends; his matronly wife had even emerged as something of a socialite. Harding and his wife traveled a good deal

together, and the senator took occasional trips alone—especially to New York.

It was in New York that Warren Harding renewed his old acquaintance with Nan Britton. Eight years before, the twelve-year-old girl—precocious, pretty, and physically mature—had often stopped in the Marion *Star* office to deliver school news to the editor. She would linger as long as possible, for she thought herself infatuated with the forty-two-year-old Harding. In 1916, when she was twenty, her father died and she moved to New York. She wrote to Senator Harding: could he help her get a job in Washington? He called on her in New York and convinced her to remain in that city. He helped her secure a job there and visited her often. Their child was born on October 22, 1919. Like so many of Harding's relationships, his affair with Nan gave him pleasure, but did great damage to his name after his death.

After World War I America was a frustrated country. Its economy was suffering through a staggering postwar inflation (which would shortly slide into a recession); its statesmen were divided over the controversial League of Nations. Senator Harding, worried that he might not be re-elected, began to speak out, and his words voiced the sentiments of the frustrated nation. What had we fought the war for anyway? What had been made safe for democracy? Certainly not Europe, which was no less troubled than it had been before the war and which was threatened with engulfment by the Red plague from Russia. Now it was America that required our attention, and Harding defined the patriot's duty: "To safeguard America first. To stabilize America first. To prosper America first. To think of America first. To exalt America first. To live for and revere America first." Americans, he said, wanted a return to "normalcy."

While Harding was trying to remind his Ohio constituents that he was clever, patriotic, and soon to be a candidate for re-election to the Senate, the Republican party was looking for a presidential nominee. The national frustration being what it was under Wilson, the proper candidate would, the party leaders estimated, have little trouble winning. And yet the leaders knew they would have to be careful: a wrong candidate, another party split like the Bull Moose disaster in 1912, and their good prospects would dissipate. They wanted a probusiness conservative and an isolationist, but at the same time someone inoffensive to labor, to the progressive wing of the party, and to those voters who might not be anti-League. Most of all they wanted someone they could "depend on"—that is, control. The ring grew crowded with hats, but there was still some shopping to be done.

Republican power was centered in the Senate. One summer day in 1919 one of the most powerful party leaders, Senator Boies Penrose, sent for Harding. "Harding," he said, "how would you like to be President?" Harding had been worrying about his chances of returning to the Senate, not of achieving the Presidency. He had no money, he protested, and he was not at all certain that he was fit for the job. "Am I a big enough man for the race?" the senator asked his mentor. "Don't make me laugh," answered Daugherty. And it was he who convinced Mrs. Harding, who was at first unreceptive to the idea, that her husband should run. Once convinced, she matched Daugherty in enthusiasm—enthusiasm that Harding never shared.

There was no Harding band wagon. The candidate did badly in primaries. He wanted to withdraw from the race, but Mrs. Harding would not let him. During discouraging times early in 1920, Harry Daugherty was quoted in *The New York Times*: "I don't expect Senator Harding to be nominated on the first, second, or third ballots, but I think we can afford to take chances that, about eleven minutes after two, Friday morning of the convention, when ten or twenty weary men are sitting around a table, someone will say, 'Who will we nominate?' At that decisive time the friends of Harding will suggest him and can well afford to abide by the result."

At the Chicago convention those men—there were actually fifteen—sent for Warren Harding and asked if there was anything in his past that might embarrass the party if he were to be its presidential candidate. There was Nan Britton, of course (who was in Chicago at that moment), and the baby, and the old Marion rumor, spread by the *Star*'s competitors, that the Hardings were part Negro; but Harding said No, Nothing. Shortly after two o'clock on Friday morning the door of the smoke-filled caucus room opened and the fifteen men emerged. Warren G. Harding would be nominated. Informed, the anointed candidate said, "Well, we drew to a pair of deuces and filled."

Boies Penrose was dying at home in Pennsylvania. He got up enough strength, however, to dispatch some advice to Republican leaders: "Keep Warren at home. Don't let him make any speeches. If he goes out on a tour somebody's sure to ask him questions, and Warren's just the sort of damned fool that will try to answer them." And home he was kept, running a front-porch campaign. In the election Harding defeated James M. Cox by seven million votes.

"Well, Warren Harding," his wife said, "I have got you the Presidency; what are you going to do with it?" Mrs. Harding was not the only person who thought herself responsible for Harding's election. Harry Daugherty thought himself responsible; Harding's Ohio cronies demanded plenty of spoils; Senator Fall of New Mexico had helped and wanted his due. Harding was not totally naïve. He knew that his mentors were not the most talented men in government, but he brought them into his administration. "God," he said, "I can't be an ingrate!"

Harding did make three outstanding appointments to his Cabinet: Charles Evans Hughes, Secretary of State; Andrew Mellon, Secretary of the Treasury; and Herbert Hoover, Secretary of Commerce. When Mellon's budget-reform program was passed in June, 1921, Harding appointed the able Charles G. Dawes director of the Budget Bureau. And he named former President Taft Chief Justice of the Supreme Court.

But for the most part, Warren Harding was baffled by the job. "I listen to one side and they seem right," he commented on one issue, "and then—God!—I talk to the other side and they seem just as right, and here I am where I started. I know somewhere there is a book that will give me the truth, but hell! I couldn't read the book." To a White House visitor he admitted: "I knew that this job would be too much for me."

While Daugherty was collecting graft, while Fall was leasing government oil to Harry Sinclair and Edward L. Doheny, while Charles Forbes of the Veterans Bureau and Thomas Miller, alien property custodian, were fattening their bank accounts at the government's expense, the President was trying to deal with the recession he had inherited. Although the deflation was checked somewhat during Harding's administration, the farmer's plight was not relieved. Harding tried unsuccessfully to produce solutions to the labor problems of 1921 and 1922, especially in the coal and railroad industries, but, to his credit, he did increase the responsibilities of the talented Herbert Hoover, whose recommendations he invariably approved. He seldom showed initiative, in part because he believed in all but unquestioning executive cooperation with Congress. He withdrew, for example, his advocacy of a department of public welfare when congressional leaders opposed it; he favored American membership in the World Court, but acquiesced to the congressional reservation that the United States should join only if

JAMES M. COX

The political background of James M. Cox, the Democratic presidential candidate in 1920, was not unlike that of his opponent, Warren G. Harding. Both men were Ohioans, both rose to prominence as journalists, and both were relatively unknown outside the Buckeye State. There the resemblance ended. In contrast to the handsome and conservative Harding, Cox was a stocky, bespectacled liberal of unimpressive appearance. A self-made millionaire, he began as a reporter and editor and eventually became the publisher of several Ohio newspapers. In 1908 he was elected to Congress, and in 1913 he began the first of two nonconsecutive terms as governor of Ohio. Cautiously progressive, he championed labor and reform without alienating conservatives, whose support proved crucial at the 1920 convention. Nominated on the forty-fourth ballot, he chose as his running mate Franklin D. Roosevelt, the young assistant secretary of the Navy. Cox's campaign lacked the dignity of his opponent's. The cocky liberal approached his audiences "a little like a frontier 'bad man' shooting up the meeting." Committed to Wilsonian progressivism and entry into the League of Nations, Cox was overwhelmingly defeated by Republican Warren G. Harding's "back to normalcy" campaign. Retiring from politics, Cox served as an American delegate to the World Monetary and Economic Conference in 1933.

the Court was totally divorced from the League of Nations; he proposed legislation that would have empowered the President to negotiate the settlement of war debts, but yielded to Congress' demands that it be the bargaining agent.

Such negotiations, however, and the signing of peace treaties with Germany, Austria, and Hungary did require some executive leadership, but this Harding left to Secretary of State Hughes. In May, 1921, Congress passed a naval appropriations bill with a rider urging the President to call an international conference to discuss naval disarmament. Hughes was placed in charge of the conference, which met in Washington on November 12. Nine different treaties were signed in all; they settled some old disagreements between the belligerents. The United States, Great Britain, France, Italy, and Japan agreed on a ten-year moratorium, during which no capital ships would be built; most of the major powers agreed to scrap some of their ships. The conference was probably the most successful venture of the Harding administration.

"God, what a job!" Harding said as his awareness of his responsibility increased. Occasionally he was guided by moral rather than political correctness. In his first year in office Harding ignored the advice of his friends and pardoned imprisoned Socialist Eugene V. Debs. "I was persuaded in my own mind that it was the right thing to do," Harding wrote in a letter to a friend. In the same letter he admitted "growing less a partisan than [he] once was." Did this mean that the President was going to rise up and do the job? For the moment, perhaps, but then he would be gripped by melancholy. One night Charles Forbes reported, "I went with the President to the rear lawn of the White House, and he cried."

Forbes, of course, was one of those then stabbing the President in the back. Late in 1922 the rumors began to circulate in government circles. Early the next year they were strong enough—and true enough—to foster two tragedies: Charles Cramer, a lawyer working with Forbes on the Veterans Bureau Frauds, shot himself to death, leaving a suicide note addressed to the President personally (Harding refused to open it); and Daugherty's Ohio associate of many years, Jesse Smith, either committed suicide or was murdered. Fall took this as a warning and resigned, thus heightening the rumors. The President began to feel the pressure: he sent Nan Britton to Europe and took a cross-country trip with Mrs. Harding. "In this job," he finally admitted as he left Washington, "I am not worried about my enemies. It is my friends that are keeping me awake nights."

Harding never returned to Washington. He died in San Francisco on August 2, 1923. A blood clot in the brain was probably the cause. (On the trip, he had suffered from heart and stomach trouble, pneumonia, and ptomaine poisoning, and he was utterly exhausted.) Mrs. Harding refused, however, to allow an autopsy. The rumors started: he had killed himself; Daugherty had killed him; Mrs. Harding had killed him. But the evidence for any death but a natural one is nonexistent. He died, one is tempted to conclude, because it was the best thing to do.

He was mourned first and then disgraced. Teapot Dome and related scandals lasted until 1927; when the investigations ended, Nan Britton published *The President's Daughter*, a plea for some of the estate for their child. (She received nothing.)

Warren Harding had been elected President because he had promised a "resumption of our onward, normal way." During his brief administration, however, a new norm emerged. Half of the American people lived in cities; cars were shrinking the country and radios were bringing America's regions still closer together. Prohibition was ignored, which reduced respect for all laws. Jazz flourished and so did the Ku Klux Klan. Babe Ruth, movie stars, and gangsters were national heroes. In this America of flappers and jelly beans, of artists who called their generation "lost," a return to normalcy was out of the question. Nothing could be returned to. Everything had changed.

—DAVID JACOBS

Warren G Harding (signature)

A PICTURE PORTFOLIO

HARDING MEMORIAL LIBRARY

The Republican National Convention of 1920 issued this medal to commemorate its nomination of Senator Warren G. Harding of Ohio for the Presidency.

A highly skilled handshaker who genuinely loved people, Warren Harding got as big a kick out of his front-porch campaign for the Presidency as did the legions of callers who journeyed to Marion, Ohio. Above: the candidate, himself an althorn player, poses with a visiting tuba. Right: callers from a Pittsburgh Republican club. Below: Harding with the entertainers Blanche Ring and Al Jolson.

The Republicans stood for "normalcy" and "order."

THE AVAILABLE MAN

As the election year of 1920 approached, the Republican party scented victory, and Harry Daugherty—Warren Harding's mentor—foresaw a dogfight for the presidential nomination. Confident that the national convention would find itself unable to agree on a candidate, Daugherty wanted to make it known that his protégé was "available," so he painted a picture of a reluctant but dedicated public servant prepared to sacrifice for his party and country. "Senator Harding," he wrote in 1919 of the onetime newspaperman, "has practically been forced into every contest for high honors he has ever received." Once the name of Warren Gamaliel Harding did emerge from the room full of smoke and party leaders, the campaign was patterned after William McKinley's. It was a front-porch campaign; Harding sat at home while his managers raised money to bring the people to visit him. Bands came to play for him and glee clubs serenaded him; Al Jolson wrote a song, which he sang enthusiastically to Harding on the candidate's front porch:

We think the country's ready
For another man like Teddy.
We need another Lincoln
To do the country's thinkin'.
(Chorus) *Mist-ter Hard-ding,*
You're the man for us! ...

BABBITT IN
THE WHITE HOUSE

President Warren G. Harding was an easy target. For the Sinclair Lewises and Sherwood Andersons, his small-town mentality and talk of a return to an impossible "normalcy" were proof that he was Babbitt in the White House. His simplistic platitudes were grist to acerb H. L. Mencken's mill. And his performance in office inspired F. Scott Fitzgerald's play *The Vegetable*, in which Jerry Frost complains: "I never asked to be President. Why—why, I don't even know how in hell I ever *got* to be President!" Warren Harding's problem was America's problem: recently urbanized, its technology creating a totally new society, the nation nevertheless still fancied itself an agrarian country and prized the old farm-and-village virtues. Harding was aware of the technological advances—he was, in fact, proud of them—but he did not understand their implications. Despite this lack of perspicacity and notwithstanding the wrath of the intellectuals, Warren Harding actually did more than any other President to preserve the Constitution of the United States. He removed that great document from the files of the State Department, where it was rotting, and put it in a protective glass case.

LIBRARY OF CONGRESS

According to contemporaries, Mrs. Harding (above), who had urged her husband to try for the Presidency, was effusive and uncertain as the First Lady.

In 1921 Harding agreed to go on a camping trip designed to show how safe automobiles were. With him at right are Henry Ford, Thomas Edison, Harvey Firestone, and Bishop William Anderson.

OHIO HISTORICAL SOCIETY

In 1922, when radio was still quite young, technology produced the radio picture. The first image to be transmitted was the face of Warren Harding (above).

Undoubtedly the most notable achievement of the Harding administration was the Washington conference on naval disarmament. At right are the delegates from Japan, England, the United States (Charles Evans Hughes), France, and Italy. Nine treaties were signed as the result of the conference, which proved that although the United States had refused to join the League of Nations, it was not completely isolationist.

George Bellows' lithograph below illustrates a phenomenon of the twenties, Billy Sunday. Thousands of people regularly looked forward to a soul-whipping by the big-league baseball player turned evangelist.

PARADOXES

The pictures on these two pages illustrate the paradoxes of American life during Warren Harding's administration. The people had endorsed Harding's campaign cry of "America first!"; yet as a powerful nation the United States could not ignore its responsibilities, and therefore a conference to limit the growth of naval armament and to discuss Far Eastern problems convened in Washington in 1921. Congress had joined the great moral crusade being waged from the nation's pulpits and had condemned Wickedness. But those who did not like prohibition went out and got drunk anyway. The President—depicted as the personification of small-town virtues—gambled, drank, and kept a mistress; but so did many other Americans. And some of those who did not wished that they did.

The accessible and ubiquitous speak-easy made prohibition tolerable, sometimes even enjoyable, for urban Americans. The painting above was one of many that Ben Shahn did on the subject of life in the twenties.

WRITERS OF THE TWENTIES

BROWN BROTHERS

F. SCOTT FITZGERALD

"Sometimes I don't know whether I'm real," remarked F. Scott Fitzgerald, "or whether I'm a character in one of my own novels." Fitzgerald was both a participant in and an ironical chronicler of the frantic twenties and the disillusioned "Lost Generation." A native of St. Paul, Minnesota, Fitzgerald left Princeton University in 1917. Three years later his first book, *This Side of Paradise*, shocked the nation by viewing "the cities between New York and Chicago as one vast juvenile intrigue" and by depicting a young America that found "all Gods dead, all wars fought, all faiths in man shaken." The novel brought fame and money to Fitzgerald and his vivacious but unstable wife, Zelda, and they lived the gay life until 1924, when because their funds had begun to run low, they moved to England. *The Great Gatsby*, a mature examination of the jaded times, was a critical success but a financial failure in 1925. Fitzgerald began writing potboilers and drinking heavily, and Zelda suffered two nervous breakdowns. *Tender Is the Night*, published in 1934, did not appeal to Depression-struck America, and Fitzgerald found himself in the "dark night of the soul," where it was "always three o'clock in the morning." He revealed his own "emotional bankruptcy" in a series of essays, *The Crack-Up*, and died in Hollywood in 1940.

HOUGHTON MIFFLIN

WILLA CATHER

Willa Cather expressed her dissatisfaction with the twenties less by overt criticism than by deft and gentle remembrances of the American past. Miss Cather was born in Virginia in 1873, but grew up in Nebraska. She had been a newspaperwoman, teacher, and magazine editor by the time her first novel, *Alexander's Bridge*, was published in 1912. It was soon followed by *O Pioneers!*, *The Song of the Lark*, *My Ántonia*, and *A Lost Lady*, all stories of people who had to live with the prairie and its "uninterrupted mournfulness." Her growing love for the American Southwest was evident in *Death Comes for the Archbishop* (1927), which, along with *Shadows on the Rock* (1931), revealed her deep interest in Roman Catholicism. Miss Cather published stories, novelettes, and essays until her death in 1947. Her style was restrained—a reflection of her love of the classics, especially Vergil. In her works many have found, as critic Clifton Fadiman put it, a "sense, touching rather than tragic, of the tears which lie in mortal things." In 1923 Miss Cather won the Pulitzer Prize for fiction for *One of Ours*, a novel that does not rank among her best works. Literary scholar William Lyon Phelps later remarked that Miss Cather was chosen because "that year her worst novel was better than everybody else's masterpiece."

THEODORE DREISER

Theodore Dreiser's novels—indictments of modern society as chaotic, purposeless, and amoral—mirrored his own struggle with the world around him. The son of poor, bigoted parents who repressed his intellectual curiosity, Dreiser left home after finishing high school. From 1892 to 1912 he was a newspaper reporter and a magazine writer and editor. His first novel, *Sister Carrie* (1900), was considered shocking and was withdrawn after its publication. Like his *Jennie Gerhardt* (1911), it portrayed sympathetically a sinful woman. In 1912 and 1914, respectively, *The Financier* and *The Titan* were published. They were part of a trilogy (completed with the posthumous publication of *The Stoic* in 1947) that dealt with a ruthless business tycoon. The villain of *An American Tragedy* (1925) was not the man who killed his pregnant sweetheart, but the society that failed to equip him with moral values. *Dreiser Looks at Russia* (1928) and *Tragic America* (1931) substituted faith in socialism for Dreiser's former negativism. Before his death in 1945, he turned to Oriental mysticism as an antidote to mechanized society. Though he has been justly criticized for his clumsy style, Theodore Dreiser was a crusading author whose naturalistic depiction of life as he saw it fostered a new and influential school of realism in American letters.

EUGENE O'NEILL

Eugene O'Neill's critics have lamented the lack of poetry and graceful writing in his plays, but the intensity and dramatic power of his works have established him as America's foremost playwright. The son of actor James O'Neill, he had worked as a gold prospector, seaman, and journalist—and had contracted tuberculosis—by the time he was twenty-four. While at a sanitarium he decided to become a dramatist, and between 1916 and 1920 ten of his one-act plays were produced. In 1920 his first full-length play, *Beyond the Horizon*, won the first of his four Pulitzer Prizes. The style of O'Neill's plays changed as his career progressed. *The Emperor Jones* and *The Hairy Ape* are expressionistic, whereas *Anna Christie* and *Desire Under the Elms* are naturalistic; all, however, are stark, tragic comments on man and his environment. In *The Great God Brown* and *Strange Interlude* O'Neill experimented with new techniques, using masks and streams of consciousness as he delved into Freudian psychology. *Mourning Becomes Electra* reset the Agamemnon legend in post-Civil War New England and won O'Neill the Nobel Prize for literature in 1936. After a period of inactivity *The Iceman Cometh* appeared in 1946. Eugene O'Neill died in 1953, but his *Long Day's Journey into Night* won a posthumous Pulitzer Prize in 1957.

In 1923 Warren Harding was a sick man. He had stomach troubles, lung troubles, heart troubles, friend troubles. As the Washington rumor mill began to churn out stories of corruption in high places—places his cronies occupied—he decided to go on a trip. He journeyed across the country and then north from Tacoma to Alaska (right). But this "voyage of understanding" provided no relief. Rather than go to bed and think about his troubles, he chose to play bridge through the night. He grew weaker, and on August 2, in San Francisco, he died. When his body was returned to the White House (below), he was mourned, but public sentiment changed because of the scandalous disclosures.

AN UNSAVORY LEGACY

Here was a man," eulogized Herbert Hoover, "whose soul was seared by a great disillusionment.... Warren Harding had a dim realization that he had been betrayed by a few of the men whom he had believed were his devoted friends. That was the tragedy of . . . [his] life. . . ." If the life was tragic, however, the death was merciful. In the second year of his administration, rumors of corruption had begun to spread, stimulating—and stimulated by—a resignation, a suicide, a mysterious death. The strain was too much for the already weak heart of the President, and he died, his own death adding fuel to the fire of rumors. When, six months later, the Walsh committee uncovered the Teapot Dome scandal and continued to find evidence of more corruption, the rumors were confirmed. Everybody told everybody else that he had told him so. Senator Henry Cabot Lodge captured the spirit of the affair in an original poem, which he read into the Congressional Record early in 1924:

Absolute knowledge have I none.
But my aunt's washerwoman's sister's son
Heard a policeman on his beat
Say to a laborer on the street
That he had a letter just last week—
A letter which he did not seek—
From a Chinese merchant in Timboctoo,
Who said that his brother in Cuba knew
Of an Indian chief in a Texas town,
Who got the dope from a circus clown,
That a man in Klondike had it straight
From a guy in a South American state,
That a wild man over in Borneo
Was told by a woman who claimed to know,
Of a well-known society rake,
Whose mother-in-law will undertake
To prove that her husband's sister's niece
Has stated plain in a printed piece
That she has a son who never comes home
Who knows all about the Teapot Dome.

When the Harding administration scandals began to be uncovered, a Memphis newspaper published the cartoon above, entitled "Assuming Definite Shape."

As the cartoon above indicates, the Republicans were in an embarrassing position in 1924; but in spite of the scandals, they kept the Presidency.

FACTS IN SUMMARY: WARREN G. HARDING

CHRONOLOGY

UNITED STATES		HARDING
Lee surrenders at Appomattox	1865	*Born November 2*
Lincoln assassinated		
Johnson impeached	1868	
Grant elected President		
Hayes elected President	1877	
Bland-Allison Act	1878	
	1879	*Enters Ohio Central College*
Garfield elected President	1880	
Garfield assassinated	1881	
Arthur becomes President		
	1882	*Moves to Marion, Ohio*
Pendleton Act	1883	
Cleveland elected President	1884	*Purchases Marion* Star *with help of friends*
Interstate Commerce Act	1887	
Harrison elected President	1888	
Sherman Antitrust Act	1890	
Sherman Silver-Purchase Act		
	1891	*Marries Florence Kling De Wolfe*
Cleveland re-elected President	1892	
McKinley elected President	1896	
Sinking of the U.S.S. *Maine*	1898	
War with Spain		
Annexation of Hawaii		
Treaty of Paris		
McKinley re-elected President	1900	
McKinley assassinated	1901	
Roosevelt becomes President		
Hay-Pauncefote Treaty		
	1902	*Elected lieutenant governor of Ohio*
Roosevelt elected President	1904	
Hepburn Act	1906	
Pure Food and Drug Act		
Taft elected President	1908	

	1910	*Loses bid for Ohio governorship*
Wilson elected President	1912	*Nominates Taft at Republican convention*
Income tax amendment adopted	1913	
Federal Reserve Act		
Federal Trade Commission Act	1914	*Elected to U.S. Senate*
Sinking of the *Lusitania*	1915	
Mexican Border Campaign	1916	*Votes against confirmation of Brandeis as Supreme Court justice*
Wilson re-elected President		*Gives keynote address at Republican convention*
War with Germany	1917	*Supports Espionage Act*
Selective Service Act		
Battle of Belleau Wood	1918	
Meuse-Argonne campaign		
World War I ends		
Eighteenth Amendment ratified	1919	
Senate refuses to ratify Treaty of Versailles	1920	*Speaks against U.S. membership in League of Nations*
Nineteenth Amendment ratified		*Elected President*
Budget and Accounting Act	1921	*Recommends emergency tariff act*
Washington Armament Conference		
Sheppard-Towner Act		
Capper-Volstead Act	1922	
Teapot Dome transactions		
Second Central American Conference		
Intermediate Credit Act	1923	*Dies August 2*

BIOGRAPHICAL FACTS

BIRTH: Blooming Grove, Ohio, Nov. 2, 1865
ANCESTRY: English and Scotch-Irish
FATHER: George Tryon Harding; b. Blooming Grove, Ohio; d. Santa Ana, Calif., Nov. 19, 1928
FATHER'S OCCUPATIONS: Farmer; physician
MOTHER: Phoebe Dickerson; b. Blooming Grove, Ohio, Dec. 21, 1843; d. May 20, 1910
BROTHERS: Charles Alexander (1874–1878); George Tryon (1878–1934)
SISTERS: Charity Malvina (1867–1951); Mary Clarissa (1868–1913); Eleanor Priscilla (1872–1878); Abigail Victoria (1875–1935); Phoebe Caroline (1879–1951)
WIFE: Florence Kling De Wolfe; b. Marion, Ohio, Aug. 15, 1860; d. Marion, Ohio, Nov. 21, 1924

CALVIN COOLIDGE

As soon as Calvin Coolidge had been nominated for Vice President in a stiflingly hot hall in Chicago in 1920, commentator H. L. Mencken of the Baltimore *Sun* "retired to the catacombs under the auditorium to soak my head and get a drink. In one of the passages," he recalled, "I encountered a colleague from one of the Boston papers, surrounded by a group of politicians, policemen and reporters. He was making a kind of speech. . . . To my astonishment I found he was offering to bet all comers that Harding, if elected, would be assassinated before he had served half his term. Some one in the crowd remonstrated gently, saying that any talk of assassination was unwise and might be misunderstood. . . . But the Bostonian refused to shut down. 'I don't give a damn,' he bawled, 'what you say. I am simply telling you what I know. I know Cal Coolidge inside and out. He is the luckiest———in the whole world!' "

The Boston journalist was only one of many observers who could find no reason other than luck for Coolidge's steady advancement. The vice presidential nominee was not physically impressive; sandy-haired, pale, thin, and tight-lipped, he could not compete with Harding's florid handsomeness. "In appearance he was splendidly null," wrote a neighbor in Massachusetts, "apparently deficient in red corpuscles, with a peaked, wire-drawn expression. You felt that he was always about to turn up his coat collar against a chilling east wind." Painfully quiet and shy, Coolidge was no backslapper. His speaking voice has been likened by several of his major biographers to a quack. He was concerned more with thrift than show: Henry Cabot Lodge is said to have remarked that any man who lived in a two-family house—as Coolidge did—was out of the question as a presidential candidate. Yet Coolidge was consistently successful in politics, and there was more to it than incredibly good

President Coolidge, in a gentle portrait by Philip de László

luck. Throughout his life he was thorough, fair, and restrained. He was a rarity in politics—a philosopher of government and an honest man, dedicated to the welfare of the community. His limitation as a statesman—he was simplistic in a variegated world—was also his strength. The electorate trusted him and frequently expressed that trust in huge majorities at the polls.

He was born in Plymouth Notch, in southern Vermont, on July 4, 1872. Then, as now, the mountainous region retained some of the character of the frontier; the rocky soil resisted cultivation and the wilderness tenaciously encroached on the farms. Plymouth's inhabitants honored old Puritan values—hard labor, self-sufficiency, and community responsibility. Emotion was seldom shown. Wit was dry and understated.

The future President was originally named after his father, John Calvin Coolidge, a farmer, storekeeper, and holder of local and state offices. Calvin—the first name was

This photograph of Coolidge as a senior at Amherst College shows him carefully dressed à la mode.

soon dropped—lived a farm boy's life: there was firewood to be split, corn to be planted, maple sap to be collected. Coolidge went to the local school, where he showed no remarkable aptitude, but at the age of thirteen he passed the examination qualifying him to teach school. He then went on to study at Black River Academy, a private school in Ludlow, twelve miles from home. Before he was eighteen, Coolidge had lost his grandfather, his mother, and his red-haired younger sister, Abbie.

Coolidge planned to enter college in the fall of 1890, but he caught a bad cold on his way to Massachusetts for the Amherst College entrance examinations and failed them. He spent the following spring term at St. Johnsbury Academy in upstate Vermont and then was admitted to Amherst on the recommendation of the principal. At college he was an "Ouden," or nonfraternity man, for the first three years; he played no sports and was only a fair student. But by his senior year diligence in study and an ability to make people laugh had given him some status in his class and confidence in himself. This confidence was enhanced immeasurably by his exposure to Charles E. Garman, professor of philosophy, who taught that Christianity, in particular Congregationalist Christianity, was superior to all other philosophical systems in the world. Garman thus rationalized for a grateful Coolidge all the things the student had been raised to believe in: hard work; consecration to the welfare of one's neighbor; the performance of good works, all of which serve God's plan. Coolidge made a fraternity his senior year; in the spring he graduated *cum laude*.

That fall he was back in the vicinity—at Northampton, only a few miles from the college—to begin studying law in the office of John C. Hammond and Henry P. Field. Almost immediately he entered politics. Henry Field was the Republican candidate for mayor of Northampton in the fall of 1895, and Coolidge served as one of his campaign workers. Field won, and in the same election John Hammond was elected district attorney. So, said Coolidge laconically, "I saw something of the working of the city government and the administration of the criminal law." He did not take undue advantage of these fortunate connections, but entered the Republican organization at the bottom. By 1897 he was a party committeeman in his ward. That year he was admitted to the bar and shortly thereafter opened an office.

Coolidge's social life consisted mostly of visits to people who made him feel at home —those who ran or frequented the barbershop, the cobbler's, the druggist's. Otherwise he kept to himself, reading and thinking. He was looked upon as an "odd stick," tight with his words, his confidences, and his money, but he was also earning a reputation as an honest worker and a faithful friend.

Then, unexpectedly, he fell in love. His choice was Grace Goodhue, "a creature of spirit, fire, and dew," wrote Alfred Pearce Dennis, "given to blithe spontaneous laughter . . . as natural and unaffected as sunlight. . . ." She was a graduate of the University of Vermont and taught at a school for the deaf in Northampton. Recognizing the contrast between them, Coolidge remarked that "having taught the deaf to hear, Miss Goodhue might perhaps cause the mute to speak." This was typical Coolidge self-deprecation, but Grace did help him with the social side of politics, providing a buffer for his sharp edges and relief from the moodiness he often displayed in public. They were married in October, 1905. Their first son, John, was born the following fall and the second, Calvin, in 1908.

By then Coolidge had risen through the posts of county court clerk, city councilman, and city solicitor and had served two terms in the state house of representatives. He continued to rise rapidly: after two terms as mayor of Northampton he was elected in 1911 to the state senate, where, three years later, he was made presiding officer. Elected lieutenant governor in 1915, he was chosen governor in 1918.

Coolidge claimed in later years that each step upward, until he became president of the state senate, was taken because it would serve the public and make him a more successful lawyer, not because he wanted a career in politics; he also liked to please his father. His ambition was tempered by his shyness. "It's a hard thing for me to play this game," he told his friend Frank Stearns. "In politics, one must meet people. . . . When I was a little fellow . . . I would go into a panic if I heard strange voices in the kitchen. . . . and the hardest thing in the world was to have to go through the kitchen door and give them a greeting. . . . I'm all right with old friends, but every time I meet a stranger, I've got to go through the old kitchen door, back home, and it's not easy."

Still, having been chosen president of the senate, he decided to try for the governorship. And, having won that post, he did well, successfully encouraging the enactment of laws prohibiting unfair practices by landlords, raising workmen's compensation allowances, and limiting the work week for women and children to forty-eight hours. He mediated labor-management arguments fairly. And he urged increases in pay for factory workers, teachers, and the Boston police force, as well as better working conditions for the police.

Had he been successful in this last effort he might never have become President. But the city government, administered by a Democratic mayor, did little to improve the policemen's lot, and by the summer of 1919 Boston's police had decided to join the American Federation of Labor. "A police officer," said Police Commissioner Edwin U. Curtis, "cannot consistently belong to a union and perform his sworn duty." Curtis suspended nineteen members of the policemen's union. Coolidge might then have moved in to mediate the potentially dangerous situation. But jurisdictions were unclear: the police commissioner was appointed by the governor (Coolidge's predecessor had named Curtis) and was more or less a law unto himself, responsible to no one. This was not just a labor-management quarrel; Coolidge would have had to mediate between government agencies, and he refused to do it. Publicly he took the position that the demands of the police were reasonable, but that they should not unionize or go out on strike—which they did on September 9, the day after the suspensions. Coolidge still preferred to leave the initiative in the hands of the local officials, but they let the situation get out of control. The night of the walkout there was looting and rioting in Boston. By the time the mayor asked Coolidge to call out part of the state guard to restore order, a general strike—one that might spread beyond Boston—seemed possible. By not acting as commander in chief of the commonwealth Coolidge was jeopardizing the peace and risking the Republican hold on the governorship, since he was up for re-election that fall. Party leaders put pressure on him, and after a tense day and a second violent night he finally took charge. He activated the rest of the guard. Curtis had been virtually replaced by an act of the mayor; Coolidge restored his power. Then, in a proclamation, Coolidge asked for the support of the public and the police. The situation quieted, and as it did, Coolidge emerged a national hero. He was a defender of the faith against "the Reds." All that was needed to cap the event was a battle cry, and soon he supplied it: "There is no right to strike against the public safety by anybody, anywhere, any time." The spark had been struck that would make him President, and he was re-elected governor by a landslide.

Frank Stearns, a Boston merchant and Amherst alumnus, had been promoting the fortunes of Calvin Coolidge since 1915. He had a collection of Coolidge's speeches (*Have Faith in Massachusetts*) published, and in 1920—while Coolidge was blocking all formal attempts to make him an active presidential candidate—Stearns sent a copy of the book to every delegate chosen to attend the Republican National Convention. At the convention a second collection of Coolidge speeches was distributed. The senators who controlled the convention dictated the presidential candidate, however, and Coolidge did not have a chance. But then the delegates rebelled: instead of choosing the anointed candidate as Harding's running mate, they backed Coolidge.

When the presidential election was over, Warren Harding set a precedent by asking Coolidge to sit as an official member of the Cabinet. But Coolidge did not excel as Vice President. His contributions to Cabinet meetings were few. Once, when asked to use his power of recognition as the Senate's presiding officer to favor the administration, thus displeasing an important senator, he avoided the duty. At the critical moment he handed the gavel to a proadministration senator, left the chamber, and returned when the deed was done. His office required him to attend social functions, and he had other opportunities to cultivate high-level politicians. But for the most part he kept to himself, even in company. "Silent Cal," the Yankee loner, was still put off by the strangers in the kitchen.

There were indications that the party might not renominate him in 1924, but "Coolidge luck" intervened. On August 2, 1923, when the Vice President was on vacation in Plymouth, Harding died in San Francisco. A few hours later Calvin Coolidge was sworn in as the thirtieth President by his father, a notary public, in the lamplit sitting room of the Coolidge home in Vermont.

Coolidge, a throwback to old American attitudes, was the ideal man to carry on Harding's promotion of "normalcy." His mode of action was thoroughly conservative. "If you see ten troubles coming down the road," he would say, "you can be sure that nine will run into the ditch before they reach you and you have to battle with only one of them."

Though his administration exuded calm, Coolidge attacked his job with characteristic thoroughness and organization. Through his office in the first few months passed experts in many fields: the members of the Harding Cabinet, liberals and conservatives, enemies and friends. All had their brains picked. Most of the ordinary problems of administration he delegated to his staff and his department heads. It is said, for example, that he once refused to read a batch of papers sent to him by Secretary of Labor James J. Davis, who wanted the President's approval of a decision he had made. "You tell ol' man Davis I hired him as Secretary of Labor," he said, "and if he can't do the job I'll get a new Secretary of Labor." He handled his first major domestic crisis the same way. When a coal strike was threatened in Pennsylvania for September 1, 1923, he talked to Commerce Secretary Herbert Hoover, the members of the U.S. Coal Commission, the head of the Interstate Commerce Commission, and Pennsylvania Governor Gifford Pinchot and dumped the responsibility in their laps. It was Pinchot who worked out the settlement.

Similarly, when the Harding scandals began to break in January, 1924, Coolidge let events more or less take their own course in Congress, although he did appoint special counsel to investigate the questionable oil leases. When the Senate demanded that Secretary of Navy Edwin Denby be asked to resign, Coolidge declared, at the insistence of two leading senators, that he would not dismiss Denby without proof of guilt—but he accepted the Secretary's resignation when Denby offered it. Pressed by Senator William E. Borah and others to fire Attorney General Harry Daugherty, Coolidge called in Borah and confronted him with Daugherty. In a painful scene the two antagonists fought the matter out while Coolidge watched silently. After Daugherty had left the room in a rage, Coolidge told Borah, "I reckon you are right." But Daugherty did not resign and Coolidge did not act even though a Senate investigation was casting dark shadows on the Attorney General's reputation. Only when Daugherty refused to allow the Senate investigators into his department's files did Coolidge ask for his resignation.

The President's policy of watchful waiting, his delegation of responsibility, his caution, and his tolerance for people who disagreed with him sometimes led to conflicts of purpose within the administration. These habits were also responsible for his lamentable failure to act decisively when he

JOHN W. DAVIS

John W. Davis, the presidential choice of the seventeen-day-long Democratic convention of 1924, was a man with exceptional ability and a straightforward manner; "the type," noted one political observer, "that street-railway conductors like to have for a superintendent—that is, 'a mighty fine man.'" A leading Wall Street corporation lawyer, Davis had formerly served as congressman from West Virginia, solicitor general of the United States for five years under President Wilson, and ambassador to Great Britain from 1918 to 1921. He was an adviser to Wilson at the peace conference at Versailles and a staunch supporter of the League of Nations. One of several favorite sons at the 1924 convention, Davis began to look attractive as a compromise candidate when the convention became hopelessly split on the issue of the Ku Klux Klan. While anti-Klan forces insisted upon New York liberal Alfred E. Smith, pro-Klan delegates continued to support William G. McAdoo. On the one hundred and third ballot Davis was nominated to break the deadlock. Running against Republican Calvin Coolidge and Progressive Robert M. La Follette, Davis was defeated in a landslide Republican victory. It was his last bid for public office. An eminently able lawyer, legislator, and diplomat, he was forgotten by his party and returned to private practice. He died in 1955, prior to his eighty-second birthday.

The sticker above is from the campaign of 1924, which featured a song promising that "when old November says 'Howdy do,'" Americans would elect Coolidge and Dawes.

saw that the stock market was getting out of hand. But they helped to win him a nomination for President in his own right. One of his first acts as President had been to appoint a skilled Southern Republican politician, C. Bascom Slemp, White House secretary. Slemp was a former congressman, a veteran dispenser of patronage and raiser of funds, and his job—which he performed successfully—was to get Coolidge a four-year term. As the Harding scandals unfolded in Congress the Democrats tried to implicate Coolidge, but he actually benefited from their charges. He handled the situation with restraint, while the Democrats, attacking a man who was obviously the epitome of honorable government, appeared vindictive. The Republicans drew together in self-defense behind Coolidge; nomination of Harding's successor began to seem the best way of demonstrating to the electorate that the corruption of individuals, not of the whole Republican party, was responsible for the disgraceful oil leases. Herbert Hoover was dispatched to California to conduct the Coolidge campaign in the state primary, in which his most formidable competitor for the nomination, Senator Hiram Johnson, was also entered. After a victory there, Coolidge won the nomination easily. Charles G. Dawes was chosen as his running mate.

Elected by a plurality of some two and a half million popular votes over the combined total of his Democratic opponent, John W. Davis, and Progressive Robert M. La Fol-

lette, Coolidge could now turn his attention to the enactment of his legislative program —such as it was. He believed that the most important product of government was good community behavior on the part of the people it served. Peace and prosperity would foster good behavior. Prosperity was undeniably linked to business, which, as he said in one of the most famous of his pithy epigrams, was America's chief business. So he maintained high tariffs to protect American industries. Regulation of business was relaxed. Federal gift taxes were eliminated, and other taxes were lowered, while the national budget and debt were sharply reduced. The result was "Coolidge Prosperity."

Unfortunately, the prosperity stood on unsteady legs—the hyperactive stock market. And when those legs trembled, Coolidge and his Secretary of the Treasury, Andrew Mellon, steadied them by public reassurances, and stock sales continued to increase. Coolidge was warned by a number of experts of the sickness of the market, and there are indications that he believed the warnings. But as he saw it, regulation of the New York Stock Exchange was the responsibility of New York State, not of the federal government. He did allow the Federal Reserve Board to try to tighten money, but in general he felt he could only sustain public confidence and hope the proper people would act to cure the sickness.

Much of the speculation depended on brokers' loans to investors; when in 1928 those loans stood at about four billion dollars, there was considerable uneasiness in the economic community over the high figure.

Therefore, in January Coolidge issued a statement saying the loans were not too great: bank deposits were on the rise, too, as were the number of securities offered for sale. Almost immediately afterward, in conversation with H. Parker Willis, an important business editor, he remarked, "If I were to give my own personal opinion about it, I should say that any loan made for gambling in stocks was an 'excessive loan.'" Willis was astonished. "I wish very much, Mr. President," he said, "that you had been willing to say that instead of making the public statement you did." Coolidge explained that he regarded himself "as the representative of the government and not as an individual" and indicated that he had simply repeated what his economic advisers had said.

Save for greasing the wheels of business, Coolidge's administration produced little effective legislation. Farmers were suffering from overproduction and poor prices, and the President vetoed two versions of the McNary-Haugen bill, which would have made the government responsible for fixing prices and selling surplus crops. Farmers, he thought, should work out their own problems.

If he was laissez-faire in domestic matters, he was an active diplomat—notwithstanding Elihu Root's remark that "he did not have an international hair in his head." Coolidge had the guidance of two excellent Secretaries of State, Charles Evans Hughes and Frank B. Kellogg. In addition he had good instincts of his own. A month after he came to office an earthquake and typhoon devastated Japan. The night he got the news, he ordered the Pacific fleet to Yokohama to help the Japanese. The good effects of this action were, however, undone by the disastrous Immigration Act of 1924, which, against Coolidge's strongly expressed wishes, included a provision banning Japanese from entry.

American relations south of the border were improved largely through Coolidge's appointment of excellent emissaries. He set a precedent when, at the invitation of the

ROBERT M. LA FOLLETTE

Robert M. La Follette, a dynamic liberal from Wisconsin, entered the 1924 election at the head of a third party called the Progressives. An attorney, he had been elected to Congress in 1884, where he served as a Republican for six years. Breaking with the party bosses, he was elected governor of Wisconsin in 1900 and instituted a progressive form of government that during his three terms became known as the Wisconsin Idea. The program included tax reforms, regulation of public utilities, direct primaries, and employment of technical experts in government. Elected to the Senate in 1906, La Follette continued to push for liberal legislation. In 1911 he drafted the platform of the National Progressive Republican League and was bitterly disappointed the next year when he lost the Progressive nomination to Theodore Roosevelt. Opposing United States entry into World War I, he was one of the "little group of willful men" who opposed many of President Wilson's goals, including membership in the League of Nations and the World Court. During the Coolidge administration he played an important part in exposing the Teapot Dome oil scandal, and his liberal following grew. In 1924 he was drafted to run for President on a new Progressive ticket and received nearly one-sixth of the votes cast. With his death the following summer, La Follette's Progressive party collapsed.

President of Cuba, he went to Havana in January, 1928, to address the Sixth Inter-American Conference.

Aside from the ban on Japanese immigration, which helped lead to war in the Pacific less than twenty years later, American foreign policy that had the greatest repercussions involved Europe and the attempts to secure a permanent peace. Germany owed a reparations debt to the Allies. The Allies, in turn, owed debts to the United States. Partly due to the high tariff, Europe did not have a large surplus of dollars with which to meet its commitments to America, and Germany was unable to keep up her payments to the Allies. Although Coolidge was unwilling either to lower tariffs or cancel the Allies' debts, American financing did maintain the status quo for a while. As Coolidge's most recent biographer, Donald R. McCoy, has put it, the two and a half billion dollars lent to Germany under the Coolidge administration's Dawes Plan for supporting the German economy "corresponded to the amounts that that country paid in reparations, which in turn corresponded to the war debt payments that the United States . . . received from its wartime allies."

Like Harding, Coolidge had to face the questions of participation in the League of Nations and improvement of the diplomatic machinery for keeping the world out of war. American membership in the League was still politically impossible, but under Coolidge the country took part in numerous League-sponsored conferences. Entry of the United States into the Permanent Court of International Justice, which President Coolidge endorsed, was prevented by the "reservationism" that had kept the United States out of the League. In 1927 Coolidge asked for a conference of the great naval powers, hoping to limit the growth of navies, but the conference was a failure. A treaty to outlaw war, worked out by Kellogg and Aristide Briand of France in 1928, was signed by sixty-two nations, but it included no provisions for enforcement.

"Coolidge's chief feat," wrote H. L. Mencken, with typical exaggeration, "was to sleep more than any other President. . . . The itch to run things did not afflict him; he was content to let them run themselves." Yet Mencken summed him up in sympathetic tones: "His failings are forgotten; the country remembers only . . . that he let it alone. Well, there are worse epitaphs for a statesman."

The country owed something else to Coolidge: at a moment when the Presidency was in danger of losing a great deal of prestige due to the Harding scandals, he reaffirmed its dignity by the honesty of his public actions. The White House, said Alice Longworth after her first post-Harding visit, had changed. "The atmosphere was as different as a New England front parlor is from a back room in a speakeasy."

The office was exhausting to him. His health and stamina were poor. And just after he had gained the signal triumph of nomination for his own term, his younger son, Calvin, died of blood poisoning. "When he went the power and the glory of the Presidency went with him," wrote Coolidge. Shortly afterward he told his father he would never again stand for public office. On August 2, 1927, the fourth anniversary of his succession, he announced, "I do not choose to run for President in 1928." Ten years, he told Senator Arthur Capper, "is longer than any other man has had it—too long!" There were other reasons, too. "Poppa says there's a depression coming," remarked Grace Coolidge, speaking of her husband. Coolidge himself said that he thought the time was near for government to become more aggressive and constructive. "I do not want to undertake it," he said.

And so he retired to Northampton and the two-family house. But his privacy was continually invaded there, and in 1930 he and Grace moved to a twelve-room home on nine acres, where he could sit in a rocker on the porch without attracting the curious. Coolidge wrote a newspaper column for a year and an autobiography. And he watched, with increasing bewilderment, the crash and the Depression. He died on January 5, 1933, of a coronary thrombosis.

—MICHAEL HARWOOD

A PICTURE PORTFOLIO

The button above, from the campaign of 1924, pro-
moted a President of whom a Northampton acquaint-
ance once said, "I had confidence in him as a shrewd
man who could not be taken in by politicians."

A POPULAR CHOICE

A hero as a result of the police strike in Boston, Coolidge was boomed for President in 1920 by many Massachusetts Republicans. He was an also-ran in the contest for the presidential nomination, but then unexpectedly became Harding's running mate. The senatorial junta that dominated the convention intended to put Senator Irvine H. Lenroot of Wisconsin on the ticket with Harding. But as Lenroot's name was being placed in nomination, many bitter delegates began to leave the hall and there were shouts of "Coolidge!" from the floor. An Oregon delegate stood on a chair and called for recognition. The chairman let him speak. Most of what he said was lost in the clatter and murmur, until the closing words: "For the exalted office of Vice President Governor Calvin Coolidge of Massachusetts!" The cheering rebels could not be halted, and Coolidge was nominated on the first ballot. The news reached him by phone. His wife, knowing how disappointed he had been at his poor showing earlier, said, "You're not going to take it, are you?" "I suppose I'll have to," Governor Coolidge answered.

Above, Massachusetts state guards remove a mob from Boston Common during the police strike in 1919. Governor Coolidge's actions to resolve the crisis, though often criticized as belated, made him a national figure.

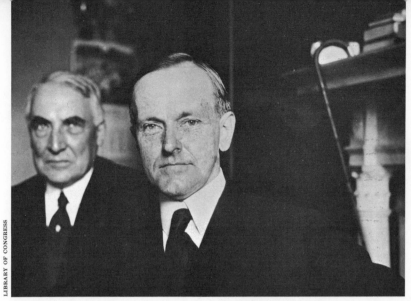

Vice President Coolidge, with Harding above, dutifully praised the President in speeches "from Maine to California, from the Twin Cities to Charleston."

On the morning of August 3, 1923, Coolidge was sworn into the Presidency by his father. (Above is a depiction of the event by Arthur I. Keller.) He said later that although in 1920 he was not sure that he could fill the office, in 1923 he "felt at once that power had been given me to administer it."

BEHIND THE MASK

A few days after Calvin Coolidge entered the White House, he wrote a brief note to Jim Lucey, the Northampton cobbler in whose shop he had passed long hours and who had advised Coolidge on many matters, from romance to politics. ". . . I want you to know," he said, "that if it were not for you I should not be here and I want to tell you how much I love you." The personality of the new President, though superficially dull, was actually complex. Coolidge had deep, suppressed emotions, a flair for wit and poetry, and a strong need to control his environment. In his home he was absolute lord; he closely supervised White House guest lists and menus and would not even let his wife in on the plans for social functions. When she protested one morning at breakfast and asked that she be given a regular list of what was scheduled, he moved his newspaper to one side just long enough to say, "Grace, we don't give out that information promiscuously." He often hid his love for her behind teasing and silence, but whenever they were separated he missed her terribly and fretted for her safety. Once, when she was late coming back from a hike, he had the Secret Service man who had accompanied her transferred and would not talk to her for days. Occasionally Coolidge revealed a distinctly poetic streak. Speaking extemporaneously at Bennington in his native state in the fall of 1928 he said, "Vermont is a state I love. I could not look upon the peaks of Ascutney, Killington, Mansfield, and Equinox, without being moved in a way that no other scene could move me. It was here that I first saw the light of day; here I received my bride, here my dead lie, pillowed on the loving breast of our everlasting hills."

Howard Chandler Christy painted the handsome portrait, at left, of Mrs. Coolidge with her white collie, Rob Roy; it still hangs in the White House.

President Coolidge is shown, left, at the White House lily pond with, from left, his elder son, John, Mrs. Coolidge, and young Calvin. The second son died of blood poisoning soon after Coolidge was nominated for his own full term. President Coolidge wrote sorrowfully: "I do not know why such a price was exacted for occupying the White House."

John Coolidge, below with Plymouth neighbors, listens to his son's acceptance speech in 1924. The President was not an exciting public speaker, and he was glad he "came in with the radio. . . . I have a good radio voice," he said, "and now I can get my message across . . . without acquainting [people] with my lack of oratorical ability. . . ."

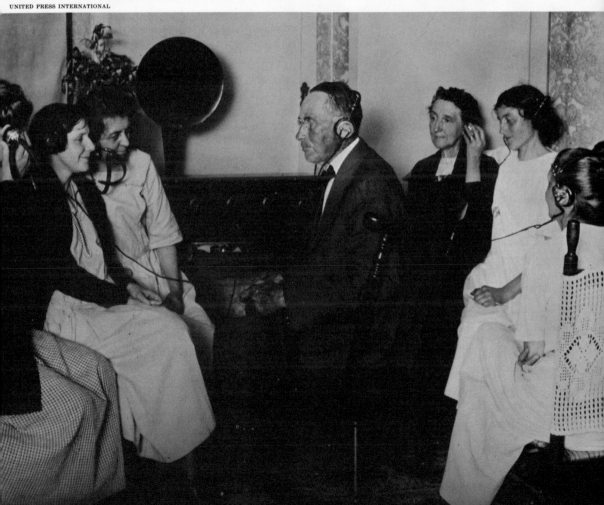

Anarchists Bartolomeo Vanzetti and Nicola Sacco (above, in a painting by Ben Shahn) were sentenced to death for a 1920 robbery-murder in Massachusetts. Despite a six-year court fight and appeals to Coolidge by many American liberals who believed the convictions reflected antialien prejudices, Sacco and Vanzetti were executed in 1927. Below, Coolidge signs the sixty-two-nation Kellogg-Briand Pact outlawing war. The United States, carrying out new and unsettling responsibilities as a world leader, had helped to initiate the treaty.

A NEW ORDER

America in the mid-twenties was caught up in a many-pronged revolution. War had ended in disillusionment. Wilson's dream of an ordered world was dead. So was American isolation. The returning servicemen, filled with cynicism and despair as a result of the brutality of battle, infused their generation with a defensive "to-hell-with-it" spirit. Sciences such as psychiatry and anthropology contributed by attacking cherished beliefs about love, the human spirit, God. Prohibition—a counter-revolution expressing a hope of man's perfectibility—was not obeyed and in the end helped overturn the old order. The Red Scare, another form of violent reaction to unusual ideas, had died down, but still smoldered, threatening ostracism of the nonconformist; its place at stage center was taken by the Ku Klux Klan, whose membership rose from practically zero in 1920 to nearly four and a half million in 1924. That same year the Democrats denied Al Smith the presidential nomination largely because he was a Catholic. Mass communication media, especially the wire services and radio, made America more of a unit than ever before; the upheaval in morals, social concepts, and religion was particularly disturbing to the country because the new communication devices allowed millions to simultaneously experience and react to it. Coolidge's response to the uneasiness was largely to ignore its symptoms while promoting, by personal example, such virtues as law and order, calmness, civic responsibility. A prewar, small-town Yankee attitude toward government, it had no chance of long-term success, but it displayed Calvin Coolidge at his best.

CHARLES G. DAWES

President Coolidge's colorful, outspoken Vice President, Charles G. "Hell and Maria" Dawes, was one of the most able statesmen of his time. Born in Ohio in 1865, he practiced law in Lincoln, Nebraska; moved to Evanston, Illinois, in 1894; and became a leading businessman, banker, and financier. Entering politics in 1896, he managed William McKinley's campaign in Illinois and was subsequently appointed comptroller of the currency. Chief procurement officer and a brigadier general during World War I, he was called upon by a postwar congressional committee to testify on military spending. Enraged at the petty nature of the investigation, he exploded in one of his famous outbursts: "*Hell and Maria*, we weren't trying to keep a set of books, we were trying to win the war!" In 1921 Dawes became the country's first director of the Bureau of the Budget. In 1924, while he served as chairman of a commission to settle the complex problems of German reparations, his Dawes Plan won him the Nobel Peace Prize. That year he was elected Vice President on the Republican ticket. Clashing head on with the Senate on the matter of rules, he gradually tempered his aggressive approach and won the respect of that body. Declining to run for re-election, he served as ambassador to Great Britain and head of the Reconstruction Finance Corporation under President Herbert Hoover. Dawes died in 1951.

NEWSMAKERS

RICHARD E. BYRD

During Richard E. Byrd's distinguished career as an explorer—begun in the twenties and spanning thirty years—he not only opened up millions of square miles of thitherto uncharted polar lands, but also proved the airplane to be a versatile instrument of exploration and scientific research. Byrd graduated from the U.S. Naval Academy in 1912 and commanded two American naval air bases in Canada during World War I. On May 9, 1926, he and his copilot, Floyd Bennett, became the first men to fly over the North Pole, for which both received the Congressional Medal of Honor. The following year Byrd headed the crew that delivered the first transatlantic mail; poor visibility forced them down in the surf off Ver-sur-Mer, but the mail got through. In September of 1928 Byrd embarked on the first of five Antarctic expeditions. He flew over the South Pole in 1929 and was made a rear admiral for this accomplishment. During a solitary encampment at an Antarctic weather station in 1934, Byrd nearly died of carbon monoxide poisoning because of a defective stove. He conducted further Antarctic explorations in 1939 and 1946, between which he performed reconnaissance in the Pacific and in Europe. Byrd's Antarctic expedition in 1955 helped United States preparations for the International Geophysical Year.

ROBERT H. GODDARD

BELIEVES ROCKET CAN REACH MOON! scoffed *The New York Times* in 1920 while reporting on an essay by Robert Hutchings Goddard, professor of physics at Clark University in Massachusetts. An early experimenter with solid-fuel rocketry, Goddard, who was a graduate of Worcester Polytechnic Institute, soon began to explore liquid propellants. On a raw day in March of 1926 he set up a steel framework to house an apparatus comprising some tubing and a few cylinders. The world's first liquid-fuel rocket rose forty feet, leveled off, and crashed less than two hundred feet away. The test did not create much of a stir, but supported by the Guggenheim Fund for the Promotion of Aeronautics, Goddard persevered. By 1928 one of his rockets soared two thousand feet into the air, and in 1935 one reached an altitude of almost a mile and a half. His work was not lost on the Germans, who patterned the V-1 rocket on Goddard's prototypes; German rocket expert Wernher von Braun later acknowledged that "Dr. Goddard was ahead of us all." During World War II Goddard directed research on naval jet aircraft and on the bazooka and made rockets that traveled seven hundred miles per hour. Goddard died in 1945 at the age of sixty-two. Fifteen years later the government paid one million dollars for the use of his patents.

CHARLES A. LINDBERGH

Charles Lindbergh, said Will Rogers, proved that "a person can still get the entire front page without murdering anybody." This quiet flyer was just the hero that an age jaded by corruption and violence needed. Raised in Minnesota, Lindbergh studied engineering and went to flying school; by 1925 he was a pilot in the Army's Air Mail Service. He decided to try for the twenty-five-thousand-dollar prize being offered for a nonstop flight to Paris and prepared by setting a transcontinental record in his monoplane, *The Spirit of St. Louis*. He took off from New York on the morning of May 20, 1927, and landed at Le Bourget Airfield in Paris thirty-three and a half hours later. At twenty-five, Lindbergh was an international idol. A parade in New York (eighteen hundred tons of shredded paper were thrown from windows in his honor) was followed by a number of successful good-will tours. After the Lindberghs' son was kidnapped and murdered in 1932, they moved to Europe. Returning in 1939, Lindbergh was rebuked by President Roosevelt for his isolationist stand, and he resigned from the Air Corps. After Pearl Harbor, however, Lindbergh supported the war effort. In 1954 he was recommissioned a brigadier general in the Air Force Reserve. His autobiography, *The Spirit of St. Louis*, won a 1954 Pulitzer Prize.

CLARENCE DARROW

"Civilization is on trial," said defense attorney Clarence Darrow during the John Scopes evolution case of 1925. And although Scopes was convicted of violating a law prohibiting the teaching of the Darwinian theory in Tennessee schools, Darrow's trenchant cross-examination of William Jennings Bryan—one of the state's lawyers—made Fundamentalism, the literal interpretation of the Bible, seem ludicrous. Darrow began his law career in Ohio and nine years later moved to Chicago, where he was active in Democratic politics and where he won wide repute as a labor counselor. He defended Eugene Debs after the Pullman strike of 1894, and in 1902 he was chief counsel for the miners on Roosevelt's arbitration commission during the Pennsylvania coal strike. After he was falsely charged (and cleared) on two counts of attempting to incite perjury, Darrow made a spectacular name for himself in criminal law. His use of psychiatric evidence averted the death penalty for child-murderers Leopold and Loeb in 1924, and his work in the notorious Massie murder case of 1932 resulted in light sentences for the four defendants. Darrow believed that even the most reprehensible criminals were entitled to counsel. He defended more than fifty persons charged with first-degree murder, but only one of Darrow's clients was executed.

WHITE HOUSE HUMOR

Calvin Coolidge, said Will Rogers, never told jokes, but "had more subtle humor than almost any public man I ever met." Rogers once invited Coolidge to a show, describing it as two or three hours of Rogers talking, plus a vocal quartet. "Yes," said Coolidge, straight-faced, "I like singing." His humor often had a bite to it, a touch of the put-down. His wife's first apple pie was less than a success, but Coolidge earnestly touted it to some of her friends, and after they had choked it down and com-plimented their embarrassed hostess, he asked, "Don't you think the road commissioner would be willing to pay my wife something for her recipe for pie crust?" In the White House he liked to press buzzers and set the staff running while he disappeared. But the President, too, was used as an object of fun. At the theater one night comedian Groucho Marx stared out at the presidential box and said to the Chief Executive, who was famous for retiring at an early hour, "Isn't it past your bedtime, Calvin?"

Vanity Fair's idea of an "Impossible Interview" linked Coolidge with the reticent actress Greta Garbo.

*The President allowed himself to be photographed
in all sorts of situations that, considering his
sphinxlike and shy demeanor, made him appear
a bit ridiculous. Above he is shown with a group
of bewigged and costumed ladies from the Jeffer-
son Memorial Commission. At right he wears a
cowboy outfit (with his nickname on the chaps),
while below, in an Indian war bonnet, he bears
more than a faint resemblance to W. C. Fields. A
friend declared that Coolidge hated being photographed, but he was probably one of the most frequently snapped men of his era. He was once
asked how he got his exercise. "Having my picture taken," he said. When some of his friends
objected to the picture of him as a cowboy because
it was making people laugh, the President re-
sponded, "Well, it's good for people to laugh."*

FACTS IN SUMMARY: CALVIN COOLIDGE

CHRONOLOGY

UNITED STATES		COOLIDGE
Grant re-elected President	1872	*Born July 4*
Hayes elected President	1877	
Garfield elected President	1880	
Garfield assassinated	1881	
Arthur becomes President		
Cleveland elected President	1884	
Presidential Succession Act	1886	*Enters Black River Academy*
Harrison elected President	1888	
	1891	*Enters Amherst College*
Cleveland re-elected President	1892	
	1895	*Graduates* cum laude *from Amherst*
McKinley elected President	1896	
	1897	*Admitted to the bar*
War with Spain	1898	*Becomes member of Northampton city council*
Treaty of Paris		
	1899	*Elected Northampton city solicitor*
McKinley re-elected	1900	
McKinley assassinated	1901	
Theodore Roosevelt becomes President		
Theodore Roosevelt elected President	1904	
	1905	*Marries Grace Goodhue*
Pure Food and Drug Act	1906	*Elected to Massachusetts house of representatives*
Taft elected President	1908	
Mann-Elkins Act	1910	*Elected mayor of Northampton*
	1911	*Elected state senator*
Wilson elected President	1912	
Federal Reserve Act	1913	
Clayton Antitrust Act	1914	*Becomes president of Massachusetts senate*
Lusitania sunk	1915	*Elected lieutenant governor of Massachusetts*
Wilson re-elected President	1916	
War with Germany	1917	
Belleau Wood	1918	*Elected governor of Massachusetts*
Meuse-Argonne Offensive		
War ends November 11		

UNITED STATES		COOLIDGE
Prohibition amendment ratified	1919	*Settles Boston police strike*
Senate rejects League of Nations		
Nineteenth Amendment ratified	1920	*Elected Vice President*
Harding elected President		
Business recession	1921	
Washington Armament Conference		
Harding dies	1923	*Becomes President*
		Sends fleet to aid victims of Japanese earthquake
Bonus bill passed over presidential veto by Congress	1924	*Wins Republican primary in California*
		Elected President
Teapot Dome scandal		*Vetoes bonus bill*
Dawes Plan		
Scopes trial	1925	
Billy Mitchell trial		
Revenue Act	1926	
Geneva Conference on Naval Disarmament	1927	*Refuses to run for re-election*
Sacco and Vanzetti executed		*Vetoes McNary-Haugen bill*
Merchant Marine Act	1928	*Issues statement saying brokers' loans were not excessive*
Hoover elected President		
		Attends Sixth Inter-American Conference in Havana
Agricultural Marketing Act	1929	*Publishes autobiography*
Stock market crash		
	1930	*Writes occasional newspaper column*
		Elected president of American Antiquarian Society
Franklin Delano Roosevelt elected President	1932	
	1933	*Dies January 5*

BIOGRAPHICAL FACTS

BIRTH: Plymouth Notch, Vt., July 4, 1872
ANCESTRY: English
FATHER: John Calvin Coolidge; b. Plymouth, Vt., March 31, 1845; d. Plymouth Notch, Vt., March 18, 192
FATHER'S OCCUPATIONS: Storekeeper; farmer
MOTHER: Victoria Josephine Moor Coolidge; b. Plymouth, Vt., March 14, 1846; d. Plymouth Notch, Vt., March 14, 1885
SISTER: Abigail (1875–1890)

WIFE: Grace Anna Goodhue; b. Burlington, Vt., Jan. 3, 1879; d. Northampton, Mass., July 8, 1957

MARRIAGE: Burlington, Vt., Oct. 4, 1905

CHILDREN: John (1906–   ); Calvin (1908–1924)

EDUCATION: Plymouth district school; Black River Academy; St. Johnsbury Academy; Amherst College

HOME: Coolidge Homestead, Plymouth Notch, Vt.

RELIGIOUS AFFILIATION: Congregationalist

OCCUPATION BEFORE PRESIDENCY: Lawyer

PRE-PRESIDENTIAL OFFICES: Member Massachusetts House of Representatives; Mayor of Northampton, Mass.; Member and President of Mass. Senate; Lt. Gov. of Mass.; Governor of Mass.; Vice President

POLITICAL PARTY: Republican

AGE AT INAUGURATION: 51

OCCUPATION AFTER PRESIDENCY: Writer

DEATH: Northampton, Mass., Jan. 5, 1933

PLACE OF BURIAL: Hillside Cemetery, Plymouth, Vt.

FIRST ADMINISTRATION

INAUGURATION: August 3, 1923; Plymouth Notch, Vt.

SECRETARY OF STATE: Charles Evans Hughes

SECRETARY OF THE TREASURY: Andrew W. Mellon

SECRETARY OF WAR: John W. Weeks

ATTORNEY GENERAL: Harry M. Daugherty; Harlan F. Stone (from April 9, 1924)

POSTMASTER GENERAL: Harry S. New

SECRETARY OF THE NAVY: Edwin Denby; Curtis D. Wilbur (from March 18, 1924)

SECRETARY OF THE INTERIOR: Hubert Work

SECRETARY OF AGRICULTURE: Henry C. Wallace; Howard M. Gore (from Nov. 22, 1924)

SECRETARY OF COMMERCE: Herbert C. Hoover

SECRETARY OF LABOR: James J. Davis

68th CONGRESS (March 4, 1923–March 4, 1925):
Senate: 51 Republicans; 43 Democrats; 2 Others
House: 225 Republicans; 205 Democrats; 5 Others

END OF PRESIDENTIAL TERM: March 4, 1925

ELECTION OF 1924

CANDIDATES	ELECTORAL VOTE	POPULAR VOTE
Calvin Coolidge Republican	382	15,718,211
John W. Davis Democratic	136	8,385,283
Robert M. La Follette Progressive	13	4,831,289

SECOND ADMINISTRATION

INAUGURATION: March 4, 1925; the Capitol, Washington, D.C.

VICE PRESIDENT: Charles G. Dawes

SECRETARY OF STATE: Frank B. Kellogg

SECRETARY OF THE TREASURY: Andrew W. Mellon

SECRETARY OF WAR: John W. Weeks; Dwight F. Davis (from Oct. 14, 1925)

ATTORNEY GENERAL: John G. Sargent

POSTMASTER GENERAL: Harry S. New

SECRETARY OF THE NAVY: Curtis D. Wilbur

SECRETARY OF THE INTERIOR: Hubert Work; Roy O. West (from Jan. 21, 1929)

SECRETARY OF AGRICULTURE: William M. Jardine

SECRETARY OF COMMERCE: Herbert C. Hoover; William F. Whiting (from Dec. 11, 1928)

SECRETARY OF LABOR: James J. Davis

SUPREME COURT APPOINTMENT: Harlan Fiske Stone (1925)

69th CONGRESS (March 4, 1925–March 4, 1927):
Senate: 56 Republicans; 39 Democrats; 1 Other
House: 247 Republicans; 183 Democrats; 4 Others

70th CONGRESS (March 4, 1927–March 4, 1929):
Senate: 49 Republicans; 46 Democrats; 1 Other
House: 237 Republicans; 195 Democrats; 3 Others

END OF PRESIDENTIAL TERM: March 4, 1929

© 1928 Life

"Mr. Coolidge refuses point-blank to leave the White House until his other rubber is found," said this cartoon by Gluyas Williams in Life magazine in 1928.